THE WIZARD OF OZ

THE
WIZARD
OF OZ

SMITHMARK

First published in England by Dragon's World Ltd, Limpsfield and
London, 1990. Published in the USA by SMITHMARK Publishers Inc.,
1993. 16 East 32nd Street, New York, NY 10016.

SMITHMARK books are available for bulk purchase for sales promotion
and premium use. For details write or call the manager of special sales,
SMITHMARK Publishers Inc., 16 East 32nd Street,
New York, NY 10016; (212) 532-6600.

Produced by Dragon's World Ltd, 26 Warwick Way,
London SW1V 1RX, England.

Editorial Assistant: Diana Steedman
Designer: Peter Ward
Editorial Director: Pippa Rubinstein

ISBN 0-8317-9462 3

Printed in Hong Kong

10 9 8 7 6 5 4 3 2 1

METRO GOLDWYN MAYER

Presents

THE WIZARD OF OZ

CONTENTS

© 1939 LOEW'S INC.

FOREWORD

It was not the first film version of L. Frank Baum's childhood classic; neither was it the last. But if you ask what *The Wizard of Oz* means today, the answer will almost certainly be an image of Judy Garland yearning to go 'somewhere over the rainbow'. Although the original book, published in 1900, and its many sequels, had a definite life of its own, most of its present celebrity would be unlikely to exist if a group of people in MGM had not, in 1939, had the inspiration to make of it the musical fantasy we know today. As close to perfect of its kind, and quite as famous as its near-contemporary *Gone With the Wind*, *The Wizard of Oz* has become a cornerstone of the Hollywood legend, a key example of what we mean when we sigh nostalgically that they don't make them like that any more.

It was not always so. Nobody realized at the time that they were making history as well as just another movie, production No 1060, and therefore no one is quite sure about how the film began, although a lot of people subsequently wanted to claim credit. The two prime contenders for the title of Wizard of *The Wizard of Oz* were both famous producers at MGM; Mervyn LeRoy and Arthur Freed. According to LeRoy he had wanted to film *The Wizard of Oz* ever since he was a child, and was finally given the chance to do so. According to Arthur Freed he was, in 1937, a young song-writer very eager to move on to bigger and better things, and one day Louis B. Mayer, head of the studio, told him to find a property suitable for musical treatment: by evening he had bought an option on the book from Samuel Goldwyn and was ready to start work. Whichever version is true, there is no doubt that Mervyn LeRoy was the credited producer on *The Wizard of Oz*, and Arthur Freed his (uncredited) assistant, on the threshold of a great career as producer of all the most famous MGM musicals of the next twenty years.

Why *The Wizard of Oz*? Why then? The book had first been filmed as early as 1910, and then unsuccessfully and quite unfaithfully, as a silent feature in 1925, with the comic Larry Semon as the Scarecrow with (the only real point of interest) a fat young man called Oliver Hardy as the Tin Woodman. Goldwyn had acquired the rights in 1934, probably meaning to use it as a vehicle for his great comic star Eddie Cantor, but had then done nothing about it. Fantasy anyway was regarded as box-office poison in the mid 1930s, but in 1937 something else was happening. Walt Disney, after a decade of making highly successful short cartoons, had gambled his future on a full-length feature, *Snow White and the Seven Dwarfs*, and the rest of Hollywood, after being profoundly sceptical, looked like having to eat its words when *Snow White* became a major box-office success. Suddenly the search was on for other fairy tales and fantasies. MGM was not the only studio to be interested in *The Wizard of Oz*: Twentieth Century-Fox thought it had possibilities as a vehicle for their own immensely popular child star Shirley Temple.

Probably when MGM bought the book and started work on it, they had no precise casting in view. First they set about getting the story into the right shape for filming. A succession of scriptwriters were brought in and thrown out. There were eleven in all, credited and uncredited, but the most important contributions seem to have been those of the young English writer Noel Langley and the man who was credited with writing the lyrics of the songs, E.Y. (Yip) Harburg. It was part of Freed's plan (and maybe LeRoy's) that the film should be a musical fantasy, and so the choice of song-writers was very important. The whole musical side of the production was left to Freed, whom LeRoy rightly considered to be the expert. And Freed had no doubts: although the thought of Jerome Kern as a possible composer flitted across his mind, he was so taken with a song called 'In the Shade of the New Apple Tree', which he felt had just the right wit, simplicity and fantasy, he decided its writers, Yip Harburg and composer Harold Arlen, were the only ones to do *The Wizard of Oz* on screen. So convinced was he that he even went along with their rather daring (though not completely new) idea of making this an integrated musical, in which each number forwarded the plot rather than being an irrelevant 'cue-for-song', with the songs arising naturally from the action and dissolving almost unnoticeably into dialogue.

Obviously, with all the special effects needed to make the fantasy convincing, this was going to be an expensive film, and so the right casting was vital. Once mooted, the idea of Shirley Temple as the artless Kansas heroine Dorothy seemed a good one; she was, after all, about the right age, and one of the biggest stars in Hollywood at the time. Unfortunately she was under contract to another studio, Twentieth Century-Fox, and they refused to lend her at any price. This gave Freed a chance to step in with his nominee from among MGM's contract players, a dumpy 15-year-old referred to with dubious affection by Louis B. Mayer as 'my little hunchback' and already known to some movie fans as Judy Garland.

Despite her plainness and puppy fat, Judy had a phenomenal voice,

full of emotion and yearning, and she projected on screen a pleasing candour, determination and vulnerability — perfect for the Dorothy Freed and Harburg had in mind. She had already made seven films, usually as the heroine's younger sister or the girl the boy regards as just a pal until the last reel, and while not quite a star, she was clearly being groomed for stardom. *The Wizard of Oz* was her big chance, and she seized it with both hands — to such an effect that ever afterwards 'Over the Rainbow' was her theme song, and even fifty years later one cannot think of one without the other. Bizarrely enough, the place of 'Over the Rainbow' in the film was not confirmed until the very last moment; it was removed and replaced several times in response to varying preview reactions, and finally reinstated only on the concerted insistence of Freed, Harburg and Arlen that it made a vital plot point and created a necessary transition from the black-and-white reality of the opening sequence to the highly coloured fantasy Oz of Dorothy's dream.

The course of great movies, like the course of true love, never does run smooth, so it is not surprising to learn that there were several hiccups in the shooting of the film, which began on 12 October 1938. The first director, Richard Thorp, was fired after two weeks, and with him went Buddy Ebsen (later the senior Beverley Hillbilly), originally cast as the Tin Woodman. The picture closed down for a week, during which George Cukor, regarded as MGM's 'women's director' *par excellence*, came in to shoot some costume and make-up tests — his major contribution being to strip off most of Judy Garland's make up and the blonde wig she had been lumbered with to reveal her own naturally dark hair. Then, by an improbable switch, Victor Fleming, regarded as MGM's 'man's director' *par excellence*, was drafted in. Some four months later, Cukor and Fleming were to stand in much the same relationship on another major movie, *Gone With the Wind*. When Cukor was fired from that, Fleming was taken off *The Wizard of Oz* to take over and placate *GWTW*'s fretful star Clark Gable; while King Vidor, who had been evading overtures to direct *Gone With the Wind*, took over *The Wizard of Oz* and shot all the Kansas sequences at the opening.

It may seem surprising that such a plethora of cooks did not produce a bungled and incoherent dish, but one has to remember that in Hollywood's heyday films were primarily a studio product, with writers, directors, and casting changing all the time, and films frequently being substantially reshot after unpromising previews and the whole thing treated as one would any other factory product. (Exactly the same thing happened with *Gone With the Wind*.) Obviously everyone had hoped and trusted that the film would be a success, but no one dreamed that it would assume the legendary status it rapidly did. Even the critics at the time were less than ecstatic: one major critic announced curtly that it was 'a stinkeroo', and most of the rest thought it was heavy-handed, lacking in humour and charm, and disfigured by Judy Garland's failure to fit into the fantastic context. On the whole

minor figures, such as vaudeville comic Bert Lahr as the Cowardly
Lion, came off best. But then, as Jack Haley, who finally played the
Tin Woodman, remarked years later, 'We didn't know it was a classic.
It was a job. We were getting paid, And it was a lot of weeks of steady
work.'

Good reviews or not, the public immediately took *The Wizard of Oz*
and Judy Garland to their hearts. If no one realized they were making
a classic, the same is happily true of *Gone With the Wind* (despite
Selznick's publicity bluster). But every now and then, out of a routine
job came one of those magic moments in movie history when the
ingredients combine in just right way. Such moments are almost by
definition unrepeatable. But that has never prevented anyone from
trying. In the case of *The Wizard of Oz*, a year later Twentieth
Century-Fox thought they could do as well or better for Shirley Temple
with a lavish version of Maeterlinck's fairy-play *The Blue Bird*. The
result was such a disaster that it virtually brought Shirley's career to
an end, and fantasy was quickly labelled box-office poison again. Nor

have later attempts at Oz been much more successful: there have been several 'returns' to Oz, an Australian rock version, and an all-black stage musical, *The Wiz*, which in 1978 was made into a spectacularly unsuccessful film, with an anything-but-little-girl Dorothy from Diana Ross.

All of which goes to prove what we knew already, that the 1939 version was very special. After all, lightning rarely strikes twice in the same place, and if later aspirants to Oz have been left wailing 'If happy little bluebirds fly beyond the Rainbow, Why, oh why can't I?' there is no satisfactory answer except that without the classic version's unique alchemy nothing works out quite right. That alchemy, alas, is a secret that only the Wizard knows, and he's not telling.

JOHN RUSSELL TAYLOR

A VICTOR FLEMING PRODUCTION

with

Judy Garland

Frank Morgan   Ray Bolger

Bert Lahr   Jack Haley

Billie Burke   Margaret Hamilton

Charley Grapewin

and

The Munchkins

Produced by MERVYN LeROY

Directed by VICTOR FLEMING

For nearly forty years this story has given faithful service to the Young in Heart; and Time has been powerless to put its kindly philosophy out of fashion.

To those of you who have been faithful to it in return

. . . and to the Young in Heart
. . . we dedicate this picture

The Wiz

The scene is a country road. Dorothy runs along with Toto following – she turns several times, looks back, then stoops down to speak to Toto. She collects up her books and runs on. Toto follows.

DOROTHY   She isn't coming yet, Toto. Did she hurt you? She tried to, didn't she? Come on. We'll go tell Uncle Henry and Auntie Em. Come on, Toto.

A farmyard. Dorothy enters along the road, followed by Toto. She runs through the gate towards Auntie Em and Uncle Henry who are working at an incubator.

DOROTHY   Aunt Em! Aunt Em!

Auntie Em and Uncle Henry are working with baby chicks. Dorothy tries to speak to them. She picks up a baby chick but Auntie Em takes it from her and returns to the coop. Dorothy follows as Auntie Em returns to incubator. Uncle Henry looks at Dorothy, who starts across the yard.

DOROTHY   Aunt Em!

AUNTIE EM   Fifty-seven, fifty-eight.

DOROTHY   Just listen to what Miss Gulch did to Toto! She –

AUNTIE EM   Dorothy, please! We're trying to count: Fifty-eight –

DOROTHY   Oh, but Aunt Em, she hit him –

UNCLE HENRY   Don't bother us now, honey. You see, this old incubator's gone bad and we're likely to lose a lot of our chicks.

DOROTHY   Oh – oh, the poor little things. Oh, but Aunt Em, Miss Gulch hit Toto right over the back with a rake just because she says he gets in her garden and chases her nasty old cat every day!

AUNTIE EM   Seventy – Dorothy, please!

DOROTHY   Oh, but he doesn't do it every day – just once or twice a week.
And he can't catch her old cat, anyway! And now she says he's going to
get the –

AUNTIE EM   Dorothy! We're busy!

DOROTHY   Oh – all right.

*Zeke, Hunk and Hickory are working on a wagon, lowering the
wagon bed in place.*

ZEKE   How's she coming?

HUNK   Take it easy.

Hunk, on the ground, gets his finger caught under the wagon bed.

HUNK   Ow! You got my finger!

ZEKE   Why don't you get your finger out of the way!

*Zeke and Hickory place the wagon bed while Hunk sits on the
ground beside the wagon. Dorothy has moved across to watch
them. Hunk hits his finger with a hammer and whirls around.*

HICKORY   There you are.

HUNK   Right on my finger!

ZEKE   It's a lucky thing it wasn't your head.

DOROTHY   Zeke, what am I going to do about Miss Gulch? Just because
Toto chases her old cat –

ZEKE   Listen honey, I got them hogs to get in.

HUNK   Now lookit, Dorothy, you ain't using your head about Miss Gulch.
You'd think you didn't have any brains at all.

DOROTHY   I have so got brains!

HUNK   Well, why don't you use them? When you come home, don't go by
Miss Gulch's place – then Toto won't get in her garden and you won't
get in no trouble. See?

DOROTHY   Oh, Hunk, you just won't listen, that's all.

HUNK   Well, your head ain't made of straw, you know.
*Zeke drives the pigs into the pen. Dorothy climbs up onto the pen
and walks along the rail while Zeke pours feed into the trough.*

ZEKE   Soo-ee! Get in there before I make a dime bank out of you! Listen
Kid, are you going to let that Old Gulch heifer try and buffalo you? She
ain't nothing to be afraid of. Have a little courage, that's all.
Dorothy walks along the railing between the pens.

DOROTHY   I'm not afraid of her.
Zeke picks up another bucket of feed – pours more into the trough.

ZEKE   Then the next time she squawks, walk right up to her and spit in
her eye. That's what I'd do.
Dorothy loses her balance and falls into the pen.

DOROTHY   Oh!

Zeke jumps into the pen and taking Dorothy's foot out of the wire, picks her up and carries her out, putting her down with Hunk and Hickory. Zeke sits down and wipes his brow.

DOROTHY   Oh! Oh, Zeke! Zeke! Zeke, get me out of here! Help! Oh!

HICKORY   Are you all right, Dorothy?

DOROTHY   Yes, I'm all right. Oh. I fell in and – and Zeke –

Dorothy, Hunk and Hickory all look at Zeke and laugh. Auntie Em enters with a plate of crullers, one for each of them.

DOROTHY   Why, Zeke, you – you're just as scared as I am!

HUNK   What's the matter, gonna let a little old pig make a coward out of you?

HICKORY   Look at you, Zeke – you're just as white –

AUNTIE EM   Here, here, what's all this jabber-wapping when there's work to be done? I know three shiftless farm hands that'll be out of a job before they know it!

HICKORY   Well, Dorothy was walking along the –

AUNTIE EM   I saw you tinkering with that contraption, Hickory. Now, you and Hunk get back to that wagon!

HICKORY   All right, Mrs Gale. But some day they're going to erect a statue to me in this town, and –

AUNTIE EM   Well, don't start posing for it now. Here, here – can't work on an empty stomach. Have some crullers.

HUNK   Gosh, Mrs Gale.

AUNTIE EM   Just fried.

HICKORY   Thanks.

HUNK   Swell.

ZEKE   You see, Dorothy toppled into the – the –

AUNTIE EM   It's no place for Dorothy about a pig sty! Now you go feed those hogs before they worry themselves into anaemia!

ZEKE   Yes, Ma'am.

DOROTHY   Auntie Em, really – do you know what Miss Gulch said she was going to do to Toto? She said she was going to –

AUNTIE EM   Now, Dorothy, dear, stop imagining things. You always get yourself into a fret over nothing.

DOROTHY Well –

AUNTIE EM Now, you just help us out today and find yourself a place where you won't get into any trouble.

DOROTHY Some place where there isn't any trouble.

Dorothy tosses a piece of cruller to Toto and leans against a haystack to sing. She walks over to a farm implement and stands by the wheel.

DOROTHY Do you suppose there is such a place, Toto? There must be. Not a place you can get to by a boat or a train. It's far, far away – behind the moon – beyond the rain –

[*sings*] Somewhere, over the rainbow, way up high
    There's a land that I heard of once in a lullaby
    Somewhere, over the rainbow, skies are blue
    And the dreams that you dare to dream really do come true . . .

Toto listens to the song, with his tail wagging. Dorothy swings on the wheel of the rake, then walks forward. Toto jumps up onto the seat and Dorothy sits on the front and pets him. She continues singing, looking up to the sky.

DOROTHY Someday I'll wish upon a star
    And wake up where the clouds are far behind me
    Where troubles melt like lemon drops
    Away above the chimney tops
    That's where you'll find me.
    Somewhere, over the rainbow, bluebirds fly
    Birds fly over the rainbow
    Why then – oh, why can't I? . . .
    . . . If happy little bluebirds fly
    Beyond the rainbow
    Why, oh, why can't I?

The scene is now a country road. Miss Gulch rides her bicycle to the gate of Gale Home. Uncle Henry comes towards her as she stops and dismounts.

MISS GULCH   Mr Gale.

UNCLE HENRY   Howdy, Miss Gulch.

MISS GULCH   I want to see you and your wife right away, about Dorothy. *Uncle Henry releases the gate he has been holding and it hits Miss Gulch.*

UNCLE HENRY   Dorothy? Well, what has Dorothy done?

MISS GULCH   What's she done? I'm all but lame from the bite on my leg!

UNCLE HENRY   You mean she bit you?

MISS GULCH   No, her dog!

UNCLE HENRY   Oh, she bit her dog, eh?

MISS GULCH   No!
The scene moves to the interior sitting room of the farmhouse. Auntie Em and Miss Gulch are seated as Dorothy enters carrying Toto. Miss Gulch tries to take Toto from Dorothy but Uncle Henry puts Toto into the basket.

MISS GULCH   That dog's a menace to the community. I'm taking him to the Sheriff and make sure he's destroyed.

DOROTHY   Destroyed? Toto? Oh, you can't! You mustn't! Auntie Em! Uncle Henry! You won't let her, will you?

UNCLE HENRY   Of course, we won't. Will we, Em?

DOROTHY   Oh, please, Aunt Em? Toto didn't mean to. He didn't know he was doing anything wrong. I'm the one that ought to be punished. I let him go in her garden. You can send me to bed without supper –

MISS GULCH   If you don't hand over that dog, I'll bring a damage suit

that'll take your whole farm! There's a law protecting folks against dogs that bite!

AUNTIE EM How would it be if she keeps him tied up? He's really gentle – with gentle people, that is.

MISS GULCH Well, that's for the Sheriff to decide. Here's his order allowing me to take him. Unless you want to go against the law.

UNCLE HENRY Uh – yes –

AUNTIE EM Now, we can't go against the law, Dorothy. I'm afraid poor Toto will have to go.

MISS GULCH Now you're seeing reason.

DOROTHY No –

MISS GULCH Here's what I'm taking him in – so he can't attack me again.

DOROTHY No, no, no! I won't let you take him! You go away! Oooh, I'll bite you myself!

AUNTIE EM Dorothy!

DOROTHY Oh, you wicked old witch! Uncle Henry, Auntie Em, don't let 'em take Toto! Don't let her take him – please!

MISS GULCH I've got an order! Let me have him!

DOROTHY Stop her!

AUNTIE EM Put him in the basket, Henry.

MISS GULCH The idea!

DOROTHY Don't, Uncle Henry. Oh, Toto!

Dorothy cries as she looks right and left, whirls around in distress. Auntie Em, Miss Gulch and Uncle Henry watch as Dorothy exits left. Auntie Em goes after her but returns and addresses Miss Gulch.

AUNTIE EM Almira Gulch, just because you own half the county doesn't mean you have the power to run the rest of us! For twenty-three years I've been dying to tell you what I thought of you! And now – well, being a Christian woman, I can't say it.

The road. Miss Gulch rides away on her bicycle and we see Toto's head peeking out of the basket on the back of the bicycle. He looks around, then jumps out and runs back down the road. Dorothy's room. Dorothy sits on the floor crying, when Toto jumps through the window onto the bed. Dorothy pets him and holds him close to her. She takes a suitcase from under the bed. Toto barks.

DOROTHY   Toto, darling! Oh, I've got you back! You came back! Oh, I'm so glad! Toto. Oh, they'll be coming back for you in a minute. We've got to get away! We've got to run away.

Footprints are seen on the dirt road as Dorothy and Toto disappear down the road away from the farmhouse. Dorothy is carrying a suitcase and basket. They walk across a bridge. Toto barks at a wagon in the gully where Professor Marvel is seen humming and busying around his wagon. Dorothy moves to the wagon which is lettered on its side:

Professor steps down from the wagon to speak to Dorothy. He crosses to a fire and gestures to Dorothy and Toto to come forward.

PROFESSOR   Well, well, well! House guests, huh? Ha ha ha ha! And who might you be? No, no, now don't tell me.

Professor sits beside the fire and Dorothy comes forward. He picks up a toasting fork.

PROFESSOR   Let's see. You're travelling in disguise. No, that's not right. You're – you're going on a visit. No, I'm wrong. You're, you're – running away.

DOROTHY   How did you guess?

PROFESSOR   Ha ha! Professor Marvel never guesses. He knows! Ha ha! Now, why are you running away?

DOROTHY   Why –

PROFESSOR   No, no, now don't tell me. They – they don't understand you at home. They don't appreciate you. You want to see other lands, big cities, big mountains, big oceans. Ha ha!

DOROTHY   Why, it's just like you could read what was inside of me.

Toto pulls a weiner off the toasting fork.

PROFESSOR   Yes.

DOROTHY   Oh, Toto, that's not polite! We haven't been asked yet.

Toto eats the weiner. Professor laughs as he puts another weiner on the toasting fork.

PROFESSOR   Ha, ha, ha! He's perfectly welcome! Ha ha! As one dog to another, huh? Ha ha ha! Here now, let's see. Where were we?

Professor puts down the toasting fork and rises.

DOROTHY   Oh please, Professor, why can't we go with you and see all the Crowned Heads of Europe?

PROFESSOR   Do you know any? Oh, you mean the thing. Yes. Well, I – I never do anything without consulting my crystal first. Let's go inside here. We'll – just come along. I'll show you.

They move inside the wagon. Dorothy and Professor enter and Professor lights the candles, sits down and puts on a turban. Dorothy moves closer to him and closes her eyes. He slips a photograph from her basket.

PROFESSOR   That's right. Here, sit right down here. That's it. Ha ha! This – this is the same genuine, magic, authentic crystal used by the priests of Isis and Osiris in the days of the Pharaohs of Egypt, in which Cleopatra first saw the approach of Julius Caesar and Mark Antony – and – and so on and so on. Now, you – you'd better close your eyes, my child, for a moment – in order to be better in tune with the infinite. We – we can't do these things without reaching out into the . . .

Professor puts the photograph of Dorothy and Auntie Em under his leg as Dorothy opens her eyes and looks into the crystal ball.
. . . infinite. Yes, that's – that's right. Now you can open them. We'll gaze into the crystal. Ah, what's this I see? A house with a picket fence – and a barn with a weather vane of a-a-running horse.

DOROTHY   That's our farm!

PROFESSOR   Oh, yes. There's – there's – there's a woman. She's – she's wearing a-a-polka-dot dress. Her face is careworn

DOROTHY   That's Aunt Em.

PROFESSOR   Yes. Her – her name is Emily.

DOROTHY   That's right. What's she doing?

PROFESSOR   Well, I – I can't see. Why, she's crying.

DOROTHY   Oh.

PROFESSOR   Someone has hurt her. Someone has just about broken her heart.

DOROTHY   Me?

PROFESSOR   Well, it's – it's someone she loves very much; someone she's been very kind to; someone she's taken care of in sickness.

DOROTHY   I had the measles once – and she stayed right by me every minute.

PROFESSOR   Uh-huh

DOROTHY   What's she doing now?

PROFESSOR   Yes, she's – what's this? Why, she's putting her hand on her heart! She's – she's dropping down on the bed!

Dorothy Oh, no! No!

PROFESSOR   Well, that's all. The crystal's gone dark.

DOROTHY   Oh, you . . . [*Dorothy picks up her basket; getting out of the wagon she picks up Toto as the Professor rises*] . . . you don't suppose she could really be sick, do you? Oh! Oh, I've got to go home right away!

PROFESSOR   But, what's this? I thought you were going along with me!

DOROTHY   Oh, no! No, I have to get to her right away! Come on, Toto! Come on! Come on!
Dorothy picks up her suitcase and runs down the path. She puts Toto down and he runs along behind her.

DOROTHY   Goodbye, Professor Marvel, and thanks a lot!
Professor runs forward to his horse and speaking into the strong wind, moves away.

PROFESSOR   Better get under cover, Sylvester! There's a storm blowin! – a whopper, to speak in the vernacular of the peasantry! Poor little kid. I hope she gets home all right.

A TWISTER HITS GALE FARM

Gale Farm. A cyclone is approaching. In the farmyard chickens run about, the wind blows weeds and dust about. Uncle Henry yells to Hunk who exits into the barn.

UNCLE HENRY   Hurry up and get them horses loose! Find Hickory! Hickory! Hickory! Doggone it! Hickory.

Zeke points to the sky while Hunk and the others drive the horses from the barn.

ZEKE   It's a twister! It's a twister!!

Auntie Em cups her hands to her mouth and calls from the corner of the house.

AUNTIE EM   Dorothy! Dorothy!

Uncle Henry, Hunk, Hickory and Zeke runs after a horse as it is turned loose.

UNCLE HENRY   Come on, everybody in the storm cellar!

Dorothy and Toto enter the yard; weeds and branches blow by; she picks up Toto and goes through the gate to the house. She opens the screen door but it blows off past her as she exits into the house. Auntie Em runs forward to Uncle Henry as they start to go into the storm cellar.

AUNTIE EM   Henry! Henry! I can't find Dorothy! She's somewhere out in the storm! Dorothy! Dorothy!

Zeke and Hunk go into the storm cellar and close the hatch after them. Inside the farmhouse Dorothy, carrying Toto, hurries from room to room calling.

DOROTHY   Auntie Em! Auntie Em! Auntie Em!

Dorothy comes out of the house and crosses to the storm cellar but unable to open the hatch, she runs back to the house.

DOROTHY   Auntie Em! Come and let me in!

Dorothy, holding Toto, looks out of the window at the storm, then turns and calls. The window blows loose and hits her on the head as it flies past. She falls down onto the bed.

DOROTHY   Auntie Em!

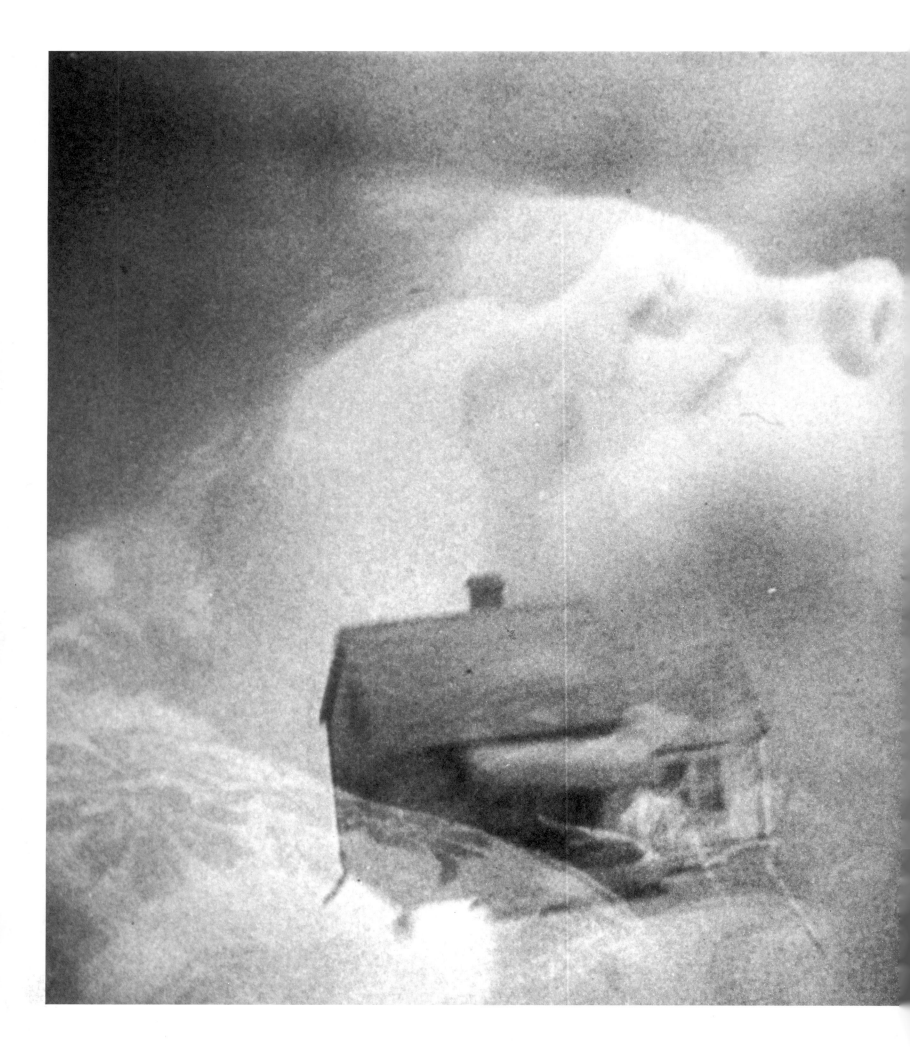

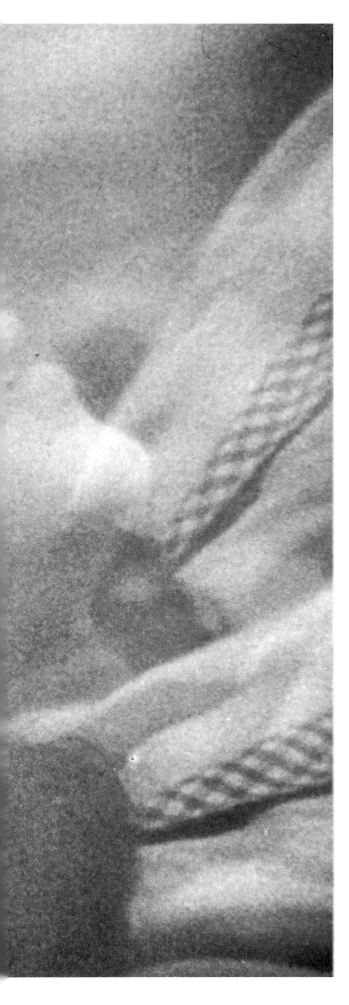

Dorothy appears to sink into subconsciousness as we see a prism shot of her superimposed with images of the whirling cyclone and the farmhouse flying through space. Dorothy is lying on the bed with Toto beside her. Objects fly past the window in the sky: a chicken roost, another house, a horse and buggy, a tree, a hen house. Dorothy wakes up and sits up to look out of the window. She and Toto peer out of the window as different objects continue to pass by: an old lady in a rocking chair passes and waves; a cow moos as it too passes by. Toto barks and jumps down from the bed away from the window. A chicken coop passes by, two men rowing a boat enter and tip their hats, then row on out of sight. Dorothy sees the swirling funnel of the cyclone.

DOROTHY   We must be up inside the cyclone!

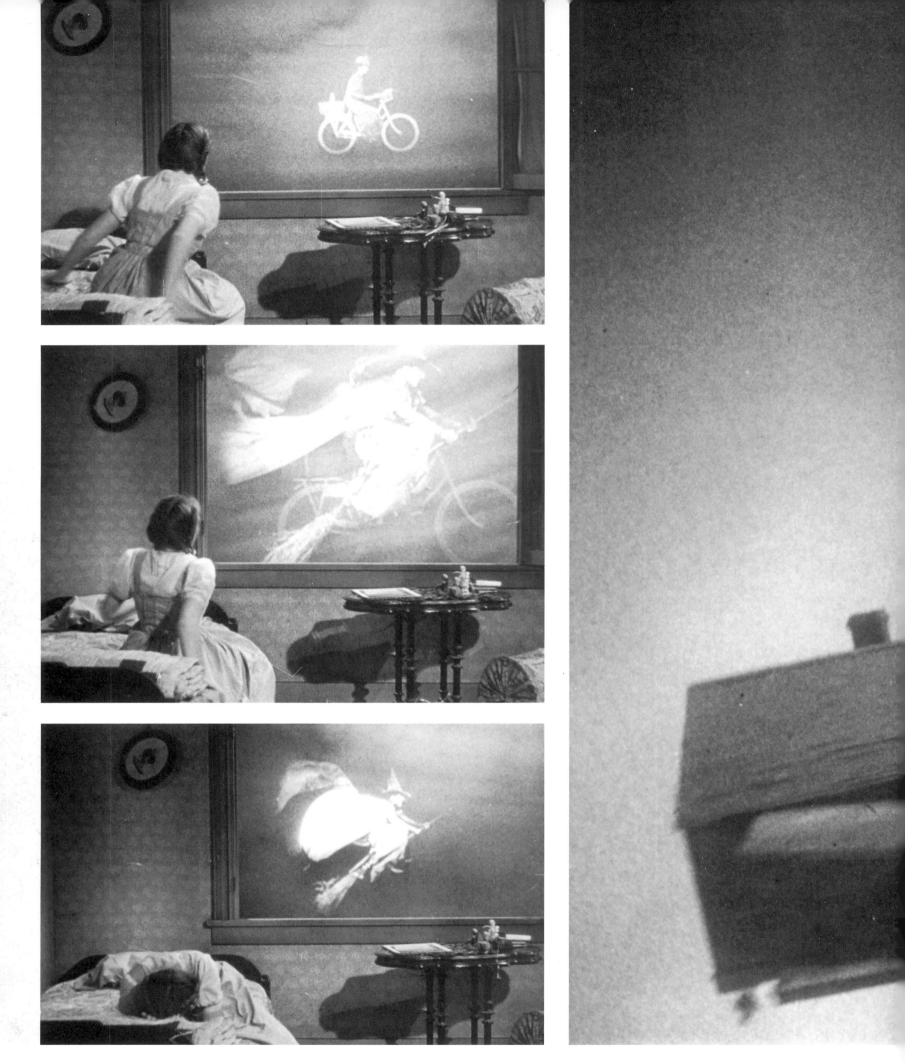

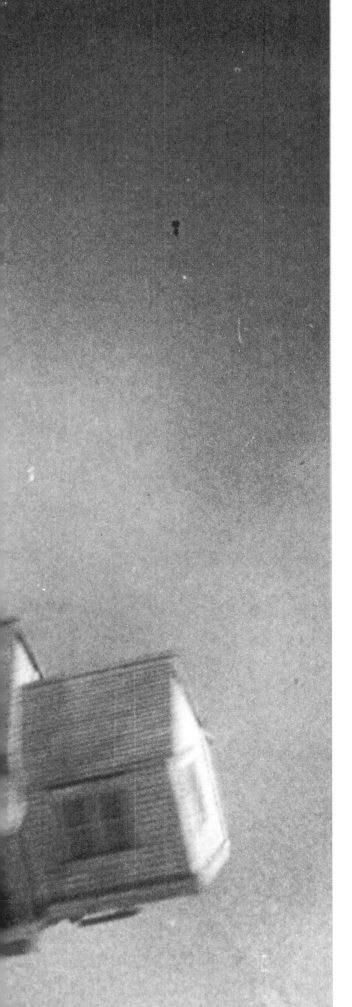

Toto peers out from underneath the bed. Pieces of wreckage continue to pass by: Miss Gulch, riding her bicycle floats into the scene and moves close to the window — her bicycle turns into a broomstick and her clothes into the flying robe and pointed hat of a witch — she moves back from the window as Dorothy hides her face in the bed.

DOROTHY   Oh, Miss Gulch!!

MISS GULCH   Ah, ha-ha-ha-ha-ha-ha-ha-ha-ha-ha!!!!

The house spins through the funnel of the cyclone downwards and is then detached. Dorothy is lying on the bed holding Toto and the bed spins and rolls around the floor with the movement of the house. Dorothy screams and the house whirls down through dust and exits below dropping into space until it comes to a crashing halt. As the dust settles, Dorothy rises with Toto in her arms, picks up her basket and opens the door to look around with startled eyes.

DOROTHY   Oh!

SOMEWHERE
OVER
THE
RAINBOW

She has opened the door of the farmhouse to reveal Munchkinland in the background. It is an array of colour. Dorothy moves towards the village square and looks about at the Civic Centre of the Munchkin Village. Munchkins can be seen hiding among the masses of flowers in the foreground – they bob up to look at her but hide away again as she turns around.

DOROTHY   Toto – I have a feeling we're not in Kansas any more. We must be over the rainbow!

Dorothy puts Toto down, onto the Yellow Brick Road, and backs away in fear as a large bubble approaches her through the air. Glinda appears out of the bubble, frightening Dorothy.

DOROTHY   Now I – I know we're not in Kansas

GLINDA   Are you a good witch, or a bad witch?

DOROTHY   Who, me! I – I'm not a witch at all. I'm Dorothy Gale, from Kansas

GLINDA   Oh! Well, is that the Witch?

DOROTHY   Who, Toto? Toto's my dog.

GLINDA   Well, I'm a little muddled. The Munchkins called me because a new witch has just dropped a house on the Wicked Witch of the East, and there's the house, and here you are, and that's all that's left of the Wicked Witch of the East.

She points to where the Wicked Witch of the East's feet can be seen protruding from beneath the farmhouse – the feet wear red slippers.

GLINDA   And so, what the Munchkins want to know is – are you a good witch or a bad witch?

DOROTHY   But I've already told you I'm not a witch at all. Witches are old and ugly. [*There is laughter all around*] What was that?

GLINDA   [*smiling*] The Munchkins. They're laughing because I am a
    witch. I'm Glinda, the Witch of the North.

DOROTHY   [*curtsies*] You are! I beg your pardon! But I've never heard of
    a beautiful witch before.

GLINDA   Only bad witches are ugly.
    The Munchkins laugh.

GLINDA   The Munchkins are happy because you have freed them from the
    Wicked Witch of the East.

DOROTHY   Oh. But – if you please, what are Munchkins?

GLINDA   The little people who live in this land. It's Munchkinland, and
    you are their national heroine, my dear. It's all right – you may all
    come out and thank her.

Munchkins appear from behind the flowers and look curiously at Dorothy.

GLINDA   [*sings*]   Come out, come out, wherever you are
       And meet the young lady, who fell from a star.
       She fell from the sky, she fell very far
       And Kansas, she says, is the name of the star

A Munchkin emerges from a manhole in the brick road.
Munchkins, singing, start off to the right.

MUNCHKINS   Kansas, she says, is the name of the star

Glinda takes Dorothy up onto a dais and the Munchkins group about them.

GLINDA   [*sings*]   She brings you good news. Or haven't you heard?
       When she fell out of Kansas a miracle occurred.

DOROTHY   [*sings*] It really was no miracle. What happened was just this.
       The wind began to switch – the house to pitch
       And suddenly the hinges started to unhitch
       Just then the Witch – to satisfy an itch
       Went flying on her broomstick, thumbing for a hitch.

A MUNCHKIN   [*sings*] And oh, what happened then was rich.

SEVERAL MUNCHKINS   [*sing*] The house began to pitch
       The kitchen took a slitch

MUNCHKINS   [*sing*]   It landed on the Wicked Witch
       In the middle of a ditch
       Which was not a healthy situation
       For the Wicked Witch

The Munchkins sing and dance.

MUNCHKINS   The house began to pitch
       The kitchen took a slitch
       It landed on the Wicked Witch
       In the middle of a ditch

Which was not a healthy . . .

A carriage drawn by ponies comes forward and pulls up in front of the dais.

MUNCHKINS [*singing*] . . ."sitch-
        Uation" for the Wicked Witch
        Who began to twitch
        And was reduced to just a stitch
        Of what was once . . .

Dorothy leaves the dais and moves to the carriage as the Munchkins assist her in getting in.

MUNCHKINS . . . the Wicked Witch [*cheering*]

Dorothy is now seated in the carriage with the driver and footman in their positions. The Munchkins step forward, singing to Dorothy, and one hands her a bouquet.

MUNCHKIN NO. 1   We thank you very sweetly
        For doing it so neatly

MUNCHKIN NO. 2   You've killed her so completely
        That we thank you very sweetly

GLINDA   Let the joyous news be spread
        The Wicked Old Witch at last is dead!

The Munchkins cheer as the carriage moves forward, followed by a procession of Munchkin soldiers. It turns and comes forward across the Civic Centre.

MUNCHKINS [*singing*] Ding Dong! The Witch is dead
        Which old Witch?
        The Wicked Witch
        Ding Dong! The Wicked Witch is dead.
        Wake up — sleepy head
        Rub your eyes
        Get out of bed
        Wake up, the Wicked Witch is dead.

The carriage moves out to exit right with the soldiers marching behind, singing.

MUNCHKINS   She's gone where the Goblins go.
        Below — below — below.
        Yo-ho, let's open up and sing
        And ring the bells out.
        Ding Dong' The merry-oh
        Sing it high
        Sing it . . .

The carriage stops at the steps of the City Hall
        . . . low
        Let them know
        The Wicked Witch is dead.

Three Heralds come out of the building. The Mayor enters after a fanfare from the trumpets, and comes forward, followed by the Barrister and the City Fathers. The Mayor approaches the carriage and helps Dorothy down from it. They both move up the

steps to the City Fathers. Dorothy and the Mayor are surrounded by the Barrister and the City Fathers.

MAYOR   [*singing*]   As Mayor of the Munchkin City
                         In the County of the Land of Oz
                         I welcome you most regally

BARRISTER   [*singing*] But we've got to verify it legally
                         To see . . .

MAYOR   To see?

BARRISTER   If she

MAYOR   If she?

BARRISTER   Is morally, ethic'lly

FATHER NO 1   Spiritually, physically

FATHER NO 2   Positively, absolutely

ALL OF GROUP   Undeniably and reliably Dead

Glinda, on the dais of the fountain, looks on and smiles. The Coroner moves up the steps towards the Mayor and Dorothy and unrolls a scroll reading Certificate of Death.

CORONER [*singing*]   As Coroner I must aver
                         I thoroughly examined her
                         And she's not only merely dead
                         She's really most sincerely dead.

Coroner, Dorothy, the Mayor, the Barrister and the City Fathers all step forward and sing.

MAYOR   Then this is a day of Independence
                         For all the Munchkins and their descendants
BARRISTER   If any.
MAYOR   Yes, let the joyous news be spread

The Mayor makes a proclamation to the Munchkins grouped about in front of the steps. They all cheer and dance.

MAYOR   The Wicked Old Witch at last is dead!
MUNCHKINS [*singing*] Ding Dong! The Witch is dead
                         Which old Witch?
                         The Wicked Witch!

The Munchkins move up the steps towards some other Munchkins sleeping in a nest. They rise, rubbing their eyes as the Munchkins sing to them. They march past huts as other Munchkins come forward from between the huts to sing and dance.

MUNCHKINS   [*singing*] Ding Dong! The Wicked Witch is dead

                Wake up, you sleepy head

                Rub your eyes

                Get out of bed

                Wake up, the Wicked Witch is dead

                She's gone where the Goblins go

                Below – below – below!

                Yo-ho, let's open up and sing

                And ring the bells out

                Ding Dong! The Merry-Oh

                Sing it high

                Let them know

                The Wicked Witch is dead!

Munchkin soldiers parade and march. Dorothy, the Mayor and other Munchkins enter on steps at the right. The soldiers line up

*before the steps as three Tots move in through the line of soldiers
and dance up to Dorothy, the Mayor and the others. The Tots
dance and sing and then exit left.*

THREE TOTS   We represent the Lullaby League

The Lullaby League, the Lullaby League

And in the name of the Lullaby League

We wish to welcome you to Munchkinland

Three Tough Kids dance forward to sing.

THREE TOUGH KIDS   We represent the Lollypop Guild, the Lollypop Guild

The Lollypop Guild

And in the name of the Lollypop Guild

We wish to welcome you to Munchkinland

They hand lollypops to Dorothy, who is standing on the steps. They dance to the other Munchkins, who then come forward to group about Dorothy, and they sing to her.

THREE TOUGH KIDS   We wish to welcome you to Munchkinland

MUNCHKINS   We welcome you to Munchkinland

Tra la la la la la la

Dorothy standing with the Mayor, the Barrister and the City Fathers, turns from one to the other as they sing.

MAYOR   From now on you'll be history.

BARRISTER   You'll be history.

CITY FATHER   You'll be history.

MAYOR   You'll be history.

GROUP   And we will glorify your name.

MAYOR   You'll be a bust.

BARRISTER   Be a bust.

CITY FATHER   Be a bust.

GROUP   In the hall of fame!

Dorothy, the Mayor and the City Fathers come forward to stand in front of Glinda on the dais. Red smoke appears and the Munchkins react to an explosion. A Witch appears out of the smoke and the Munchkins scatter, prostrating themselves on the ground in fear.

The Wicked Witch of the West (Miss Gulch) looks about at the Munchkins and waves her broomstick. Dorothy, terrified with fear as she sees Miss Gulch, hugs Toto close to her. Miss Gulch moves over to the farmhouse to look at the Wicked Witch of the East.

DOROTHY   I thought you said she was dead.

GLINDA   That was her sister – the Wicked Witch of the East. This is the Wicked Witch of the West. And she's worse than the other one was. *The Wicked Witch (Miss Gulch) turns away from the farmhouse and addresses Dorothy.*

MISS GULCH   Who killed my sister? Who killed the Witch of the East? Was it you?

DOROTHY   No, no. It was an accident. I didn't mean to kill anybody.

MISS GULCH   Well, my little pretty, I can cause accidents too!

GLINDA   Aren't you forgetting the ruby slippers?

MISS GULCH   The slippers – yes!

Miss Gulch turns to the farmhouse, looks down at the Wicked Witch of the East's feet protruding from beneath the house.

MISS GULCH   The slippers!

The Witch of the East's legs protrude from beneath the house but the slippers disappear and the legs are drawn back under the house.

MISS GULCH   They're gone!

Miss Gulch rises from her position next to the house and points at Dorothy's feet.

MISS GULCH   The ruby slippers! What have you done with them? Give them back to me or I'll –

GLINDA   It's too late! There . . .

Glinda's wand points to the slippers.

GLINDA   . . . they are, and there they'll stay!

DOROTHY   [*gasps*] Oh!

MISS GULCH   Give me back my slippers! I'm the only one that knows how to use them. They're of no use to you. Give them back to me. Give them back!

GLINDA   Keep tight inside them. Their magic must be very powerful or she wouldn't want them so badly.

Miss Gulch threatens Dorothy. Glinda laughs.

MISS GULCH   You stay out of this, Glinda, or I'll fix you as well!

GLINDA   [*laughs*] Oh, rubbish! You have no power here. Be gone before somebody drops a house on you, too!

MISS GULCH   Very well, I'll bide my time – and as for you, my fine lady, it's true I can't attend to you here and now as I'd like, but just try to stay out of my way – just try! I'll get you, my pretty, and your little dog, too! [*laughs*]

Miss Gulch backs away from Dorothy and Glinda and laughs menacingly. Munchkins hug the ground with fear. Miss Gulch disappears in a cloud of fire and smoke and the Munchkins cry out.

GLINDA It's all right. You can get up. She's gone.

The Munchkins all rise, and start to move towards Glinda and Dorothy on the dais.

GLINDA It's all right. You can all get up.

The Munchkins crowd about the two. Glinda and Dorothy step down from the fountain dais.

GLINDA Pooh – what a smell of sulphur! I'm afraid you've made rather a bad enemy of the Wicked Witch of the West. The sooner you get out of Oz altogether, the safer you'll sleep, my dear.

DOROTHY Oh, I'd give anything to get out of Oz altogether, but — which is the way back to Kansas? I can't go the way I came.

GLINDA No, that's true. The only person who might know would be the great and wonderful Wizard of Oz himself.

The Munchkins bow as Glinda mentions the Wizard.

DOROTHY The Wizard of Oz? Is he good or is he wicked?

GLINDA Oh, very good, but very mysterious. He lives in the Emerald City and that's a long journey from here. Did you bring your broomstick with you?

DOROTHY No, I'm afraid I didn't.

GLINDA   Well, then, you'll have to walk. The Munchkins will see you safely to the border of Munchkinland. And remember, never let those ruby slippers off your feet for a moment, or you will be at the mercy of the Wicked Witch of the West.

DOROTHY   But – how do I start for the Emerald City?

GLINDA   It's always best to start at the beginning – and all you do is follow the Yellow Brick Road.
Glinda kisses Dorothy on the forehead before Dorothy walks through the Munchkins to the start of the Yellow Brick Road.

DOROTHY   But – what happens . . . [*Glinda dissolves into a large bubble, which floats away. The Munchkins yell, and run after the bubble, waving goodbye.*] . . . if I –

GLINDA   Just follow the Yellow Brick Road.

MUNCHKINS   Goodbye, Goodbye!
Dorothy looks up open-mouthed with astonishment. She starts to follow the Yellow Brick Road — the Mayor steps in and speaks to her as do the Munchkins.

DOROTHY   My! People come and go so quickly here! Follow the Yellow Brick Road. Follow the Yellow Brick Road.

MAYOR   Follow the Yellow Brick Road.

FIRST MUNCHKIN   Follow the Yellow Brick Road.
WOMAN   Follow the Yellow Brick Road.
BARRISTER   Follow the Yellow Brick Road.
The Munchkins line the border of the road and sing while Dorothy walks around the road.

FIDDLERS   Follow the Yellow Brick Road.
                        Follow the Yellow Brick Road,
                        Follow, follow, follow, follow,
                        Follow the Yellow Brick Road.
                        Follow the Yellow Brick Road
                        Follow the Yellow Brick
                        Follow the . . .
Dorothy comes forward down the Yellow Brick Road – Munchkins on both sides of the road sing to her, then follow her forward down the road. Dorothy passes through the gates and exits, while the Munchkins stop at the gates.
FIDDLERS   [*singing*] . . . Yellow Brick
                        Follow the Yellow Brick Road

                        You're off to see the Wizard
                        The Wonderful Wizard of Oz
                        You'll find he is a whiz of a Wiz!
                        If ever a Wiz! there was.
                        If ever oh ever a Wiz! there was
                        The Wizard of Oz
                        Is one because
                        Because, because, because, because, because

                      Because of the wonderful things he does.
          Dorothy dances down the Yellow Brick Road. She turns, waves as
          the Munchkins cheer.
FIDDLERS   [*sing*]   You're off to see the Wizard
                       The Wonderful Wizard of Oz

FOLLOW THE YELLOW BRICK ROAD

The scene is now the crossroads of Yellow Brick Road. Dorothy and Toto come along the road. She pauses in the centre of the crossroads and looks about.

DOROTHY   Follow the Yellow Brick Road? Follow the Yellow Brick . . .?
She is puzzled as she looks about.

DOROTHY   Well, now which way do we go?
A Scarecrow (Hunk) is on a pole in the cornfield at the right – he speaks, pointing to the right. Dorothy whirls about.

HUNK   Pardon me. That way is a very nice way.

Dorothy, a bit frightened as she looks about, looks down at Toto. He barks.

DOROTHY   Who said that?
Toto barks at the scarecrow.

DOROTHY   Don't be silly, Toto. Scarecrows . . . [*The Scarecrow points to the left with his other arm*] . . . don't talk.

HUNK   It's pleasant down that way, too.

DOROTHY   That's funny. Wasn't he pointing the other way?

HUNK   Of course, people do go . . . [*Hunk crosses his arms and points in both directions.*] . . . both ways!

DOROTHY   Why – you did say something, didn't you?
Dorothy steps forward to the cornfield as she speaks to Hunk. Hunk shakes his head, then nods.

DOROTHY   Are you doing that on purpose, or can't you make up your mind?

   The Scarecrow (Hunk) shows his straw head.

HUNK   That's the trouble. I can't make up my mind. I haven't got a brain, only straw.

DOROTHY   Well, how can you talk if you haven't got a – brain?

HUNK   I don't know. But some people without brains do an awful lot of talking, don't they?

DOROTHY   Yes, I guess you're right.

   Dorothy steps over the fence and into the cornfield.

DOROTHY   Well, we haven't really met properly, have we?

HUNK   Why no.

DOROTHY   [*curtsies*]   How do you do?

HUNK   How do you do?

DOROTHY   Very well, thank you.

HUNK   Oh, I'm not feeling at all well. You see, it's very tedious being stuck up here all day long with a pole up your back.

DOROTHY   Oh, dear – that must be terribly uncomfortable. Can't you get down?

Dorothy moves around to the back of the pole to help him.

HUNK   Down? No, you see, I'm – well, I'm –

DOROTHY   Oh, well, here – let me help you.

HUNK   Oh, that's very kind of you – very kind.

Dorothy tries to unfasten Hunk.

DOROTHY   Oh, dear – I don't quite see how I can –

HUNK   Of course, I'm not bright about doing things, but if you'll just bend the nail down in back, maybe I'll slip off and –

DOROTHY   Oh . . . [*Hunk slips down from the post*] . . . yes.

HUNK   Ohhhh!

Hunk drops to the ground, straw falling out of him.

HUNK   [*laughing*] Whoops! There goes some more of me again!

DOROTHY   Oh. Does it hurt you?

HUNK   Oh, no. I just keep picking it up and putting it back in again. My! It's good to be . . . [*Hunk whirls around and falls over a broken down fence. Dorothy screams and rushes forward to him*] . . . free!

DOROTHY   [*screams*] Ohhh!

HUNK   Did I scare you?

DOROTHY   No, no I – I just thought you hurt yourself.

HUNK   But I didn't scare you?

DOROTHY   No, of course not.

HUNK   I didn't think so.

Hunk and Dorothy are seated on the ground when a crow flies in and perches on Hunk's shoulder.

HUNK   Boo! Scat! Boo!

The crow picks a piece of straw from Hunk's shoulder and then flies away with it.

HUNK   You see, I can't even scare a crow. They come from miles around just to eat in my field and — and laugh in my face. Oh, I'm a failure, because I haven't got a brain!

DOROTHY   Well, what would you do with a brain if you had one?

Hunk starts to sing. Dorothy helps him to his feet and holds him when he starts to fall.

HUNK   Do? Why, if I had a brain, I could —

[*sings*]   I could while away the hours
Conferrin' with the flowers
Consultin' with the rain
And my head I'd be scratchin'
While my thoughts were busy hatchin'
If I only had a brain
I'd unravel every riddle
For any individ'le
In trouble or in pain

DOROTHY   [*sings*]   With the thoughts you'll be thinkin'
You could be another Lincoln
If you only had a brain!

HUNK   [*sings and dances*]   Oh, I could tell you why
The ocean's near the shore
I could think of things I never thunk before
And then I'd sit — and think some more.
I would not be just a nothin'
My head all full of stuffin'
My heart all full of pain . . .
. . . I would dance and be merry
Life would be a ding-a-derry
If I only had a brain.

DOROTHY   Ohh!

Dorothy stuffs straw into his coat as she speaks to him.

DOROTHY   Wonderful! Why, if our scarecrow back in Kansas could do that, the crows'd be scared to pieces!

HUNK   They would?

DOROTHY   Yes.

HUNK   Where's Kansas?

DOROTHY   That's where I live. And I want to get back there so badly, I'm going all the way to the Emerald City to get the Wizard of Oz to help me.

HUNK   You're going to see a Wizard?

DOROTHY   Um-hmm.

HUNK   Do you think if I went with you this Wizard would give me some brains?

DOROTHY   I couldn't say. But even if he didn't you'd be no worse off than you are now.

HUNK   Yes, that's true.

DOROTHY   But maybe you'd better not. I've got a Witch mad at me, and you might get into trouble.

HUNK   Witch? Huh! I'm not afraid of a Witch! I'm not afraid of anything – oh, except a lighted match.

DOROTHY   I don't blame you for that.

HUNK   But I'd face a whole box full of them for the chance of getting some brains. Look – I won't be any trouble, because I don't eat a thing, and I won't try to manage things, because I can't think. Won't you take me with you?

DOROTHY   Of course, I will.

Dorothy stands up. Hunk jumps up in the air, almost falls, so Dorothy holds him. Toto watches as Dorothy and Hunk sing and dance down the Yellow Brick Road.

HUNK   Hooray! We're off to see a Wizard!

DOROTHY   Oh – well, you're not starting out very well.

HUNK   Oh, I'll try! Really, I will.

DOROTHY   To Oz?

HUNK   To Oz!

DOROTHY AND HUNK   [*singing*] We're off to see the Wizard
The Wonderful Wizard of Oz
We hear he is a whiz of a Wiz!
If ever a Wiz' there was
If ever oh ever a Wiz' there was
The Wizard of Oz is one because
Because, because, because,
       because, because,
Because of the wonderful things he
       does
We're off to see the Wizard
The Wonderful Wizard of Oz!

WE'RE OFF
TO SEE
THE
WIZARD

Dorothy and Hunk move along the Yellow Brick Road. Miss Gulch hides behind an apple tree. She slinks down and exits left. Dorothy and Hunk stop to look at the apple trees.

DOROTHY   Oh, apples! Oh – look! Oh!

Dorothy reaches up to pick an apple off the tree – the tree reaches out and takes the apple away from her, slapping her hand.

DOROTHY   Ouch!

TREE   What do you think you're doing?

Dorothy addresses the first tree.

DOROTHY   We've been walking a long way, and I was hungry and – did you say – something?

FIRST TREE   She was hungry!

SECOND TREE   She was hungry!

The two trees gesture.

FIRST TREE   Well, how would you like to have someone come along and pick something off of you?

Dorothy looks at Hunk several times.

DOROTHY   Oh dear! I keep forgetting I'm not in Kansas.

HUNK   Come along, Dorothy – you don't want any of those apples. Hmm!

FIRST TREE   Are you hinting my apples aren't what they ought to be?

HUNK   Oh, no! It's just that she doesn't like little green worms!

FIRST TREE   Oh, you!

First Tree grabs Dorothy. She screams and struggles loose and runs out right. The trees gesture as Hunk waves at them as he runs out right.

HUNK   I'll show you how to get apples.

First Tree throws an apple and hits Hunk who falls to the ground. First tree throws another apple.

HUNK   Hooray! I guess that did it! Help yourself.

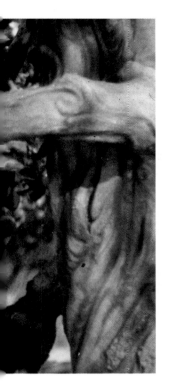

Hunk and Dorothy move through the foliage picking up apples. Toto runs about. Dorothy notices a tin foot and raps on it. It is the Tin Man (Hickory).

DOROTHY   Why, it's a man! A man made out of tin!

HUNK   What?

DOROTHY   Yes, Oh – look!

HICKORY   Oil can! Oil can!

DOROTHY   Did you say something?

HICKORY   Oil can!

DOROTHY   He said oil can.

HUNK   Oil can what?

DOROTHY   Oil can? Oh!

HICKORY   Ahh!

DOROTHY   [*picking up oil can*] Here it is!

    Hickory tries to speak. Hunk and Dorothy oil him about the mouth.

DOROTHY   Where do you want to be oiled first?

HICKORY   My mouth – my mouth!

HUNK   He said his mouth! The other side!

DOROTHY   Yes – there.

    Hickory moves his mouth as the joints squeak.

HICKORY   Me – e, me – e –

    Dorothy oils his arm. She hands the oil can to Hunk so he may oil the other arm.

HICKORY   My – m – my, my, my, my goodness, I can talk again! Oh – oil my arms, please – oil my elbows. Oh! Oh!

DOROTHY   Here.

HICKORY   Oh! Oh!

DOROTHY   Oh.

Dorothy straightens Hickory's arm as Hunk oils the other arm.

HICKORY   Oh! Oh!

DOROTHY   Oh.

HICKORY   Oh!

DOROTHY   Did that hurt?

HICKORY   No, it feels wonderful. I've held that axe up for ages. Oh!

DOROTHY   Oh, goodness! How did you ever get like this?

HICKORY   Oh – well, about a year ago, I was chopping that tree . . . [*While they speak they work Hickory's joints. Dorothy raps on his chest and Hickory hits himself on the chest and staggers backwards*] . . . when suddenly it began to rain.

DOROTHY   Oh!

HICKORY   And right in the middle of a chop, I – I rusted solid. And I've been that way ever since. Oh.

DOROTHY   Well, you're perfect now.

HICKORY   My – my neck. My – my neck. Perfect? Oh – bang on my chest if you think I'm perfect. Go ahead – bang on it!

HUNK   Beautiful! What an echo!

HICKORY   It's empty. The tinsmith forgot to give me a heart.

DOROTHY AND HUNK   No heart!

HICKORY   No heart!

DOROTHY   Oh.

HICKORY   All hollow.

Hickory falls back against the tree as Dorothy and Hunk move to
help him. He holds them off and starts to sing.

HICKORY   When a man's an empty kettle
He should be on his mettle
And yet I'm torn apart
Just because I'm presumin'
That I could be kind-a-human
If I only had a heart

I'd be tender – I'd be gentle
And awful sentimental
Regarding Love and Art
I'd be friends with the sparrows . . .
. . . And the boy who shoots the arrows
If I only had a heart
Picture me – a balcony
Above a voice sings low

SNOW WHITE'S VOICE   Wherefore art thou, Romeo?

HICKORY   I hear a beat – how sweet!
> Just to register emotion
> Jealousy – Devotion
> And really feel the part
> I could stay young and chipper
> And I'd look it with a zipper
> If I only had a heart . . . !

Hickory moves forward slightly as Dorothy and Hunk follow but his joints stick so Hunk and Dorothy oil them. He bows and starts to dance, tapping his chest and blowing a whistle through his funnel hat. Dorothy and Hunk look at each other in amazement at Hickory's antics. Dorothy whispers to Hunk. Hickory dances forward slightly and folds his arms but they lock in that position. Hickory leans to the left and right as they run back and forth to keep him from falling. As they hold him, Hunk staggers backwards and falls to the road. Dorothy grabs Hickory's hand and oils his arm.

DOROTHY   Oh, oh . . .

HICKORY   Oh.

DOROTHY   . . . oh, oh, oh, are you all right?

HICKORY   I'm afraid I'm a little rusty yet. Oh.

DOROTHY   Oh, dear. That was wonderful! You know, we were just wondering why you couldn't come with us to the Emerald City to ask the Wizard of Oz for a heart.

HICKORY   Well, suppose the Wizard wouldn't give me one when we got there?

DOROTHY   Oh, but he will! He must! We've come such a long way already.

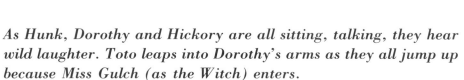

As Hunk, Dorothy and Hickory are all sitting, talking, they hear wild laughter. Toto leaps into Dorothy's arms as they all jump up because Miss Gulch (as the Witch) enters.

MISS GULCH   You call that long? Why, you've just begun. Helping the little lady along, are you, my fine gentlemen? Well, stay away from her! [*She points to Hunk*] or I'll stuff a mattress with you!

Hickory, Dorothy, holding Toto, and Hunk react as Hickory points to Hunk and then to himself.

MISS GULCH   And you! I'll use you for a bee-hive! Here, Scarecrow! Want to play ball?

Miss Gulch is standing on the roof of a house, and throws a ball of fire at Hunk. As he jumps back she laughs.

HUNK   Oh!

Hunk jumps around wildly as fire burns in front of him. He falls to the ground as Hickory puts out the fire.

HUNK   Oh! Look out! Oh, I'm burning! I'm burning! Oh!

Miss Gulch laughs wildly and waves her broom, disappearing in a cloud of smoke. As the smoke clears away Hunk rises from the ground.

HUNK   I'm not afraid of her. I'll see you get safely to the Wizard now, whether I get a brain or not! Stuff a mattress with me – hah!

HICKORY   I'll see you reach the Wizard, whether I get a heart or not. Bee-hive – bah! Let her try and make a bee-hive out of me!

DOROTHY   Oh, you're the best friends anybody ever had. And it's funny, but I feel as if I'd known you all the time. But I couldn't have, could I?

HUNK   I don't see how. You weren't around when I was stuffed and sewn together, were you?

HICKORY   And I was standing over there rusting for the longest time.

DOROTHY   Still, I wish I could remember. But I guess it doesn't matter anyway. We know each other now, don't we?

HUNK   That's right.

HICKORY   We do.

HUNK   To Oz?

HICKORY   To Oz!

Hunk, Dorothy and Hickory sing and dance.

THREE   We're off to see the Wizard
     The Wonderful Wizard of Oz
     He is – he is a whiz of a wiz!
     If ever a wiz there was
     If ever – oh ever a wiz there was
     The Wizard of Oz is one because
     Because, because, because, because, because
     Because of the wonderful things he does
     We're off to see the Wizard
     The Wonderful Wizard of Oz!

LIONS, AND TIGERS AND BEARS

The scene moves to the interior of the dark and eerie Forest.
Hickory, Dorothy and Hunk walk down the brick road, stopping
and reacting to sounds and moving slowly forward.

DOROTHY   I don't like this forest! It's – it's dark and creepy!

HUNK   Of course, I don't know, but I think it'll get darker before it gets
lighter.

DOROTHY   Do – do you suppose we'll meet any wild animals?

HICKORY   Mmm – we might.

DOROTHY   Oh –

HUNK   Animals that – that eat straw?

HICKORY   A – some – but mostly lions, and tigers, and bears.

DOROTHY   Lions!

HUNK   And tigers!

HICKORY   And bears!

  They look all around them.

DOROTHY   Oh! Lions, and tigers, and bears! Oh, – my –

DOROTHY, HICKORY AND HUNK   Lions and tigers and bears!

DOROTHY   Oh, my!

HUNK   [*pointing right*] Oh, look!

DOROTHY   Oh!

  Zeke (as the Cowardly Lion) appears and growls, moving forward
  slightly as the others jump back. Dorothy hides behind a tree as
  Hunk and Hickory fall to the ground. Dorothy peeks from behind
  the tree as Zeke growls. He rises and holds up his paws.

ZEKE   Hah! Put 'em up! Put 'em – up! Which one of you first? I'll fight
you both together, if you want. I'll fight ya' with one paw tied behind
my back! I'll fight ya' standin' on one foot!

  Zeke moves over to Hickory.

ZEKE   I'll fight ya' with my eyes closed. Oh, pullin' an axe on me eh? Sneakin' up on me, Eh? Why! [*snarling*]

HICKORY   Here – here. Go way and let us alone.

ZEKE   Oh, scared, huh?

Dorothy peeks from behind the tree.

ZEKE   Afraid, huh?

Zeke laughs at Hickory's reaction.

ZEKE   Hah! How long can you stay fresh in that can? Come on, get up and fight, you shivering junk yard! Put your hands up, you lop-sided bag of hay!

HUNK   Now that's getting personal, Lion.

HICKORY   Yes, get up and teach him a lesson.

HUNK   Well, what's wrong with you teachin' him?

HICKORY   A – well – well, I hardly know him.

ZEKE   Well. I'll get you . . . [*Toto jumps into the foliage and barks*] . . . anyway, Pee-Wee.

Dorothy reacts to Zeke's attack and picks Toto up in her arms as Zeke looks for him in the underbrush. Zeke growls and runs towards Dorothy but when she slaps his face, he starts to cry.

DOROTHY   Oh! Shame on you!

ZEKE   What did you do that for? I didn't bite him.

DOROTHY   No, but you tried to.

Dorothy, holding Toto in her arms, chastises Zeke who begins to cry, wiping his eyes with his tail.

DOROTHY   It's bad enough picking on a straw man, but when you go around picking on poor little dogs.

ZEKE   Well, you didn't have to go and hit me, did you? Is my nose bleedin'?

DOROTHY   Well, of course not. My goodness, what a fuss you're making! Well, naturally when you go around picking on things weaker than you are – why, you're nothing but a great big coward!

ZEKE   You're right, I am a coward! [*crying*] I haven't any courage at all. I even scare myself. Look at the circles under my eyes.

Zeke wipes his eyes with his tail.

ZEKE   I haven't slept in weeks.

HICKORY   Why don't you try counting sheep?

ZEKE   That doesn't do any good – I'm afraid of 'em.

HUNK   Oh, that's too bad. Don't you think the Wizard could help him, too?

DOROTHY   I don't see why not. Why don't you come along with us? We're on our way to see the Wizard now. To get him a heart.

HICKORY   And him a brain.

DOROTHY   I'm sure he could give you some courage.

ZEKE   [*crying*] Well, wouldn't you feel degraded to be seen in the company of a cowardly lion? I would.

DOROTHY   No, of course not!

Dorothy wipes his eyes with a handkerchief.

ZEKE   Gee, that – that's awfully nice of you. My life has been simply unbearable.

DOROTHY   Oh, well, it's all right now. The Wizard'll fix everything.

ZEKE   It – it's been in me so long, I just gotta tell you how I . . . [*Dorothy sets Toto down on the ground. Zeke sings, as the four walk and dance along the brick road*] . . . feel.

DOROTHY   Well, come on!

ZEKE   Yeh, it's sad, believe me, Missy
   When you're born to be a sissy
   Without the vim and verve
   But I could show my prowess
   Be a lion not a mou-ess
   If I only had the nerve
   I'm afraid there's no denyin'
   I'm just a dandelion
   A fate I don't deserve
   I'd be brave as a blizzard

HICKORY   I'd be gentle as a lizard –

HUNK   I'd be clever as a gizzard –

DOROTHY   If the Wizard is a Wizard who will serve
  They all sing.

HUNK   Then I'm sure to get a brain –

HICKORY   A heart –

DOROTHY   A home –

ZEKE   The nerve.

  Hunk, Hickory, Dorothy and Zeke dance arm in arm.

ALL   [*sing*] Oh, we're off to see the Wizard
   The Wonderful Wizard of Oz
   We hear he is a whiz of a Wiz'
   If ever a wiz there was . . .

  They sing and dance arm in arm down the Yellow Brick Road.
   . . . If ever, oh ever, a wiz' there was
   The Wizard of Oz is one because
   Because, because, because, because, because
   Because of the wonderful things he does
   We're off to see the Wizard
   The Wonderful Wizard of Oz!

The images of Hunk, Hickory, Dorothy and Zeke appear in a crystal ball as they continue to march along the brick road arm in arm. Miss Gulch and Nikko look into the crystal – she cackles as she mixes a poison. She holds the poison over the crystal and waves her hand. The images of the group fade out and a poppy field fades in.

MISS GULCH A-hah! So, you won't take warning, eh? All the worse for you, then! I'll take care of you now instead of later! Hah! When I gain those ruby slippers, my power will be the greatest in Oz! And now, my beauties! Something with poison in it, I think. With poison in it, but attractive to the eye and soothing to the smell! Poppies! Poppies! Poppies will put them to sleep.

Hunk, Hickory, Dorothy and Zeke walk out of the forest and into the poppy field.

MISS GULCH Sleep – now they'll sleep.

DOROTHY [*pointing*] There's Emerald City! Oh, we're almost there at last! At last!

Beyond the poppy field, the Emerald City is a fine view.

DOROTHY It's beautiful, isn't it? Just like I knew it would be. He really must be a wonderful Wizard to live in a city like that!

ZEKE Well, come on, then. What are we waiting for?

They run through the poppies.

HUNK Nothing! Let's hurry!

DOROTHY Yes, let's run!

HUNK Come on – come on!

HICKORY Hurry! Hurry!

Dorothy lags behind but Hunk hollers and gestures as he sees the Emerald City ahead.

HUNK   Oh, look! Come on!

HICKORY   It's wonderful! The Emerald City!

Dorothy runs through the poppies, up to Zeke, Hickory and Hunk.

DOROTHY   Oh – oh – what's happening? What is it? [*She puts her hand to her forehead*] . . . I can't run any more. I'm so sleepy.

HUNK   Here, give us your hands and we'll pull you along.

DOROTHY   Oh no, please. I have to rest for just a minute. Toto . . . [*Toto is asleep on the grass*] . . where's Toto?

Dorothy lies down in the poppies.

HUNK   Oh, you can't rest now. We're nearly there.

Hickory starts to cry. Zeke, Hickory, Hunk kneel beside Dorothy but Zeke starts to yawn and lie down. Hickory and Hunk hold him up. They move forward to pick up Dorothy but Zeke falls down among the poppies.

HUNK   Don't cry – you'll rust yourself again!

ZEKE   Come to think of it, forty winks wouldn't be bad.

HUNK   Don't you start it, too!

HICKORY   No! We ought to try and carry Dorothy.

HUNK   I don't think I could, but we could try.

HICKORY   Let's.

HUNK   Yes.

HICKORY   Oh – now look at him! This is terrible!

HUNK   Here, Tin Man – help me.

HICKORY   Oh!

Dorothy sleeps in the poppies.

HUNK   Uh. Oh, this is terrible! I can't budge her an inch! This is a spell, this is!

HICKORY   It's the Wicked Witch! What'll we do? HELP! HELP!

HUNK   It's no use screaming at a time like this. Nobody will hear you! HELP!

Hickory and Hunk holler from the hilltop. The Good Witch appears above them waving her wand, when snow begins to fall.

HUNK   HELP! HELP! Help! It's snowing!

As the snow falls, Hunk jumps wildly about.

HUNK   No, it isn't! Yes, it is! Oh, maybe that'll help! Oh, but it couldn't help!

As the snow falls, Dorothy rises and opens her eyes. Zeke sits up.

HUNK   It does help! Dorothy, you're waking up!

DOROTHY   Oh, Oh.

ZEKE   Ah-ah. Unusual weather we're having, ain't it?

DOROTHY   [*pointing to Hickory*] Look, he's rusted again! Oh, give me the oil can, quick! Oh!

HUNK   Here! Oil him.

Dorothy oils Hickory's joints.

DOROTHY Oh.

ZEKE He is rusted.

DOROTHY Here.

ZEKE Here.

DOROTHY Oil him!

ZEKE Oil him!

DOROTHY Quick . . .!

The scene moves to the interior of the Tower Room where Miss Gulch glowers into the crystal as the images of the group fade. She gestures and throws something.

MISS GULCH   Oh, Curses! Curses! Somebody always helps that girl! But shoes or no shoes, I'm still great enough to conquer her. And woe to those who try to stop me!

Outside on the hilltop, Zeke, Hickory, Dorothy and Hunk hear voices singing.

DOROTHY   Come on, let's get out of here. Look – Emerald City is closer and prettier than ever!

VOICES   You're out of the woods
        You're out of the dark
        You're out of the night
        Step into the sun
        Step into the light
        Keep straight ahead for
        The most glorious place on the . . .

Zeke, Dorothy, Hickory and Hunk skip arm in arm through the poppies, to the Emerald City.

VOICES   . . . Face of the earth or the sky
        Hold onto your breath
        Hold onto your heart
        Hold onto your hope
        March up to the gate
        And bid it open.

Back in the Tower Room, Miss Gulch and Nikko are seen. She waves her broom in the air, snarling, and then jumps into space.

MISS GULCH   To the Emerald City as fast as lightning!

Miss Gulch screams wildly as she flies on her broomstick.

IN THE MERRY OLD LAND OF OZ

Hunk, Dorothy, Hickory and Zeke approach the Gate of the Emerald City.

VOICES   [*singing*] You're out of the woods
                  You're out of the dark
                  You're out of the night
                  Step into the sun
                  Step into the light
                  March up to the gate
                  And bid it open – open.

Dorothy rings the bell. A window in the door opens and the Professor sticks his head through the little window in the door.

PROFESSOR   Who rang that bell?

HUNK, DOROTHY, HICKORY AND ZEKE   We did!

PROFESSOR   Can't you read?

HUNK   Read what?

PROFESSOR   The notice!

HUNK, DOROTHY, HICKORY AND ZEKE   What notice?

PROFESSOR   It's on the door as plain as the nose on my face! It's a – Oh –
oh – oh – oh.

*Professor disappears inside the castle – reappearing, he hangs a
sign on the door and shuts the window. Dorothy points to the
words on the sign.*

DOROTHY, ZEKE, HUNK AND HICKORY   Bell out of order – please knock.
They knock.

PROFESSOR   [*reappearing*] Well, that's more like it. Now, state your
business.

DOROTHY, ZEKE, HUNK AND HICKORY   We want to see the Wizard.

PROFESSOR   Oh – oh – the Wizard? A – but nobody can see the great Oz!
Nobody's ever seen the Great Oz! Even I've never seen him!

DOROTHY   Well then, how do you know there is one?

PROFESSOR   Because – he's a b – I – Oh – you're wasting my time!

DOROTHY   Oh – Oh, please. Please, sir. I've got to see the Wizard. The
Good Witch of the North sent me.

PROFESSOR   Prove it!

HUNK   She's wearing the ruby slippers she gave her!
Professor leans out of the window to look.

PROFESSOR   Oh – so she is! Well, bust my buttons! Why didn't you say
that in the first place! That's a horse of a different colour! Come on in!
*As the gate opens for them, Dorothy, Zeke, Hickory and Hunk
enter to find people moving about on the Street of Oz. The
Professor enters in a cab drawn by a White Horse.*

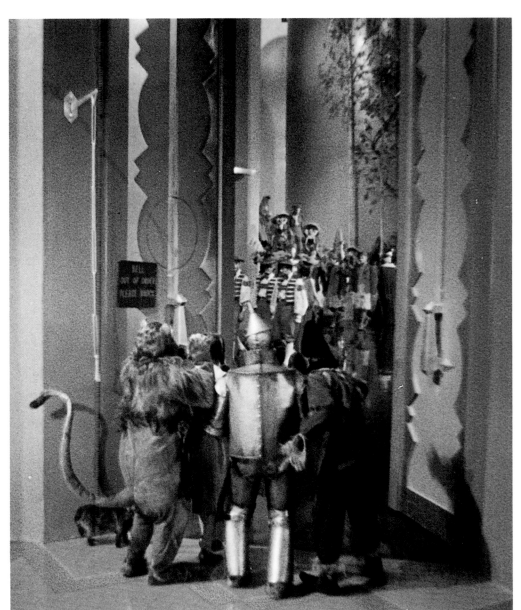

PROFESSOR   Cabby! Cabby! Just what you're looking for! Take you any place in the City, we does!

DOROTHY   Well, would you take us to see the Wizard?

PROFESSOR   The Wizard! The Wizard! I – I – Well, yes, – of course, but first I'll take you to a little place where you can tidy up a bit – what? *Dorothy, Zeke, Hickory and Hunk climb up into the cab and the Professor drives forward. People on each side of the street wave.*

DOROTHY   Oh, thank you so much. We've been gone such a long time, and we feel so mess – What kind of a horse is that? I've never seen a horse like that before!

PROFESSOR   No – and never will again, I fancy. There's only one of him, and he's it. He's the Horse of a Different Colour, you've heard tell about.

[*sings*] Ha – ha – ha –
Ho – ho – ho –
And a couple of tra – la – las
That's how we laugh the day away
In the Merry Old Land of Oz!

Bzz – bzz – bzz
Chirp – chirp – chirp
And a couple of la – di – das . . .

Professor drives the cab through the street, now drawn by a Red Horse People gather around, waving.

PROFESSOR [*sings*] . . . That's how the crickets crick all day
In the Merry Old Land of Oz.
We get up at twelve . . .
. . . and start to work at one
Take an hour . . .

Professor drives the cab through the Street of Oz, drawn by a Yellow Horse. As the cab stops, Dorothy, Hunk, Hickory and Zeke get out of the cab and exit into a building showing a sign above the door.

PROFESSOR AND CHORUS [*sing*]
That's how we laugh the day away
. . . for lunch
And then at two we're done.

Jolly good fun!
Ha – ha – ha
Ho – ho – ho
And a couple of tra la – las
That's how we laugh the day away
In the Merry Old Land of Oz!
Ha – ha – ha
Ho – ho – ho
Ha – ha – ha – ha
That's how we laugh the day away
With a ho – ho – ho
Ha – ha – ha
In the Merry Old Land of Oz!

In the Wash & Brush Up Company three men work on Hunk, filling him with new straw – they sing as they work. Other men polish and oil Hickory, and girls work on Dorothy. Other girls clip Zeke and they all sing.

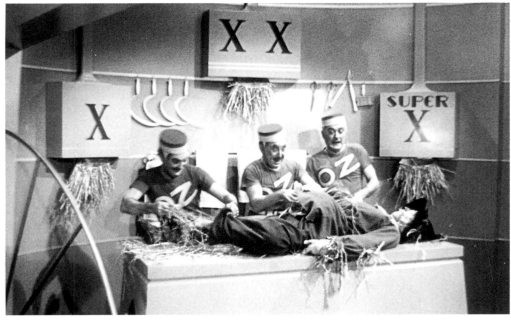

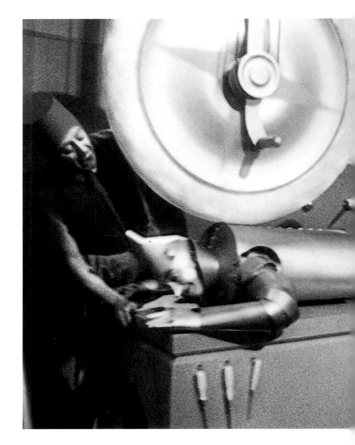

MEN   [*singing*]   Pat, pat here
Pat, pat there
And a couple of brand new straws
That's how we keep you young and fair
In the Merry Old Land of Oz.

POLISHERS   [*sing*]   Rub, rub here
Rub, rub there
Whether you're tin or brass
That's how we keep you in repair
In the Merry Old Land of Oz!

GIRL   [*sings*] We can make a dimple smile out of a frown –
DOROTHY   [*sings*] Can you even dye my eyes to match my gown?
GIRL   Uh-huh!
DOROTHY   Jolly Old town!

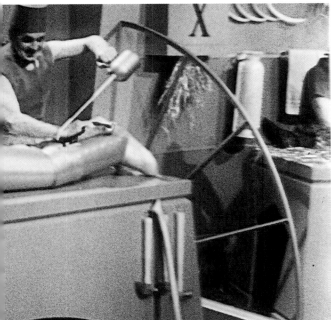

MANICURISTS	[*sing*]	Clip, clip here
		Clip, clip there
		We give the roughest claws
ZEKE	[*sings*]	That certain air of savoir faire
		In the Merry Old Land of Oz!
HUNK		Ha – ha – ha –
HICKORY		Ho – ho – ho –
DOROTHY		Ho – ho – ho – ho –
ALL	[*sing*]	That's how we laugh the day away
		In the Merry Old Land of Oz!
		That's how we laugh . . .

Dorothy and group come out into the Street after their treatment, all singing.

> . . . the day away Ha – ha – ha –
> Ha – ha – ha – ha – ha – ha
> Ha – ha – ha – ha – ha – ha
> In the Merry Old Land of Oz!
> Ha – ha – ha – Ho – ho – ho

They all stop and look up to the sky to see Miss Gulch, the Wicked Witch, riding through the sky on her broomstick with black smoke trailing behind her forming the letters: S U R R – she laughs and gestures

ZEKE Who's her? Who's her?

DOROTHY It's the Witch! She's followed us here!

Smoke writes in the sky to read: SURRENDER DOROTHY.

TWO OZ WOMEN [*looking up to the sky*] Dorothy? Who's Dorothy? The Wizard will explain it!

MAN To the Wizard! To the Wizard!

DOROTHY Whatever shall we do?

HUNK Well, we'd better hurry if we're going to see the Wizard!

Dorothy and the group run out to the right, with the crowd following. The Professor greets them at the steps of the Palace, as the townspeople rush up to him.

PROFESSOR Here – here! Everything is all right. Stop that now – just – Every – it's all right! Everything is all right! The Great and Powerful Oz has got matters well in hand – I hope – and so you can all go home! And there's nothing to worry about.

Dorothy, Hunk, Zeke and Hickory make their way through the crowd up to the Professor.

PROFESSOR   Get out of here now – go on! Go on home, and I – I – Go home.

DOROTHY   If you please, sir. We want to see the Wizard right away. All – four of us.

PROFESSOR   Orders are – Nobody can see the Great Oz! Not nobody – not nohow!

DOROTHY   Oh, but – but please. It's very important.

ZEKE   And – and I got a permanent just for the occasion.

PROFESSOR   Not nobody – not nohow!

HUNK   But she's Dorothy!

PROFESSOR   [*reacting*] The Witch's Dorothy? Well – that makes a difference. Just wait here – I'll announce you at once!
Professor turns to the Palace door and the group go up the steps of the terraced garden.

HUNK   Did you hear that? He'll announce us at once! I've as good as got my brain!

HICKORY   I can fairly hear my heart beating.

DOROTHY   I'll be home in time for supper!

ZEKE   In another hour I'll be King of the Forest. Long live the King!
[*singing*] If I were King of the Forest,
      Not Queen, not Duke, not Prince . . .
Dorothy, Hunt and Hickory move forward to listen to him.
      . . . My regal robes of the forest
      Would be satin,
      Not cotton, not chintz.
      I'd command each thing
      Be it fish or fowl
      With a woof and a woof
      And a Royal growl – woof.
      As . . .

. . . I'd click my heel
All the trees would kneel
And the Mountains bow
And the bulls kowtow . . .
And the sparrow would take wing
If I – If I – were King!
Each rabbit would show respect . . .
. . . to me
The chipmunks genuflect to me
Though my tail would lash
I would show compash
For every underling
If I – If I – were king!
Just King!

Hunk and Hickory roll a green carpet down the steps and Dorothy walks forward as a Flower Girl. Hunk and Hickory pick up the royal robe to put it on Zeke. Dorothy and Hunk hold the robe as Zeke marches up the steps. Hickory walks with him, then breaks one of the flower pots to make a crown, which he places on Zeke's head.

ZEKE   [*singing*] Monarch of all I survey
                 Mo--na-a-a---a-arch
                 Of all I survey!

Hunk and Dorothy bow to Zeke. Zeke and Hickory come forward to Dorothy and Hunk and all four walk forward to the steps of the Palace.

DOROTHY   Your Majesty, If you were King
            You wouldn't be afraid of anything?
ZEKE   Not nobody, now nohow!
HICKORY   Not even a rhinocerous?
ZEKE   Imposserous!
DOROTHY   How about a hippopotamus?
ZEKE   Why, I'd thrash him from top to bottomamus!
DOROTHY   Supposin' you met an elephant?
ZEKE   I'd wrap him up in cellophant!
HUNK   What if it were a brontosarurus?
ZEKE   I'd show him who was King of the Fores't
ALL   How?
ZEKE   How?

      Courage!
      What makes a King out of a slave?
      Courage!
      What makes the flag on the mast to wave?
      Courage!
      What makes the elephant charge his tusk
      In the misty mist, or the dusky dusk
      What makes the muskrat guard his musk?
      Courage!

    Zeke speaks and gestures
      What makes the sphinx the seventh wonder?
      Courage!
      What makes the dawn come up like thunder?
      Courage!
      What makes the Hottentot so hot?
      What puts the "ape" in apricot?
      What have they got that I ain't got?

ALL   Courage!

ZEKE   You can say that again, Huh?

Professor comes out of the Palace, shouts and exits back into the Palace, closing the door.

PROFESSOR   Go home! The Wizard says go away!

ALL   Go away?

DOROTHY Oh –

HUNK Looks like we came a long way for nothing.

DOROTHY Oh, and I was so happy! I thought I was on my way home.

HICKORY Don't cry, Dorothy. We're . . . [*Professor appears at the opening of the door, unseen by the group*] . . . going to get you to the Wizard.

HUNK We certainly are.

Dorothy cries. Hickory, Zeke and Hunk try to comfort her.

DOROTHY Auntie Em was so good to me, and I never appreciated it. Running away – and hurting her feelings. Professor Marvel said she was sick. She may be dying and – and it's all my fault.

Professor can be seen at the window, crying, the tears running down his face.

DOROTHY I'll never forgive myself! Never – never – never!

Professor, at the door, sobs and then the doors to the Palace open slowly. Dorothy, Hunk, Zeke and Hickory rise and start forward into the long corridor.

PROFESSOR [*crying*] Please don't cry any more. I'll get you into the Wizard somehow. Come on. I had an Aunt Em myself once!

THE GREAT AND POWERFUL OZ

Zeke, Dorothy, Hunk and Hickory walk forward cautiously, stopping several times to keep Zeke from running back – they clasp hands.

ZEKE   Wait a minute, fellows. I was just thinkin' – I really don't want to see the Wizard this much. I better wait for you outside.

HUNK   What's the matter?

HICKORY   Oh, he's just scared again.

DOROTHY   Don't you know the Wizard's going to give you some courage?

ZEKE   I'd be too scared to ask him for it.

DOROTHY   Oh – well then, we'll ask him for you.

ZEKE   I'd sooner wait outside.

DOROTHY   Why? Why?

ZEKE   Because I'm still scared!

DOROTHY   Oh, come on.

ZEKE   OHHH!

HUNK   What happened!

ZEKE   Somebody pulled my tail!

HUNK   Oh, you did it yourself!

ZEKE   I – Oh –

HUNK   Here. Come on.

PROFESSOR'S VOICE   Come forward!
    Zeke puts his paws over his eyes.
ZEKE   Tell me when it's over!
    Hickory, Dorothy, Zeke and Hunk move down the long corridor to the interior of the Throne Room. They enter and move to the centre of the room. They all react as they see smoke flare from the throne. Zeke tries to leave.

ZEKE   Oh, look at that! Look at that! Oh – oohhh-hhh! I want to go home!
    As the flames flare up, an ethereal image of the Wizard of Oz
    appears above the throne.

OZ'S VOICE   I am Oz, the Great and Powerful!
    Hunk, Zeke, Dorothy and Hickory watch, trembling with fear.

OZ'S VOICE   Who are you? Who are you?
    Dorothy, Hunk, Zeke, Hickory and Toto all react with fear.
    Dorothy is shoved forward.

DOROTHY   I – If you please, I – I am Dorothy – the small and meek. We've
    come to ask you –

OZ'S VOICE   Silence!

DOROTHY   Oh! . . . [*She runs back to the other three*] . . . Ohh – Jiminy
    Crickets!

OZ'S VOICE   The Great and Powerful Oz knows why you have come. Step
    forward, Tin Man!
    Hickory shakes with fear, groaning as he steps forward.

HICKORY   Ohhh!

OZ'S VOICE   You dare to come to me for a heart, do you? You clinking, clanking, clattering collection of calig- . . . [*Hickory trembles with fear*] . . . inous junk!

HICKORY   Ohhh – yes – yes, sir – Y-Yes, Your Honour. You see, a while back, we were walking down the Yellow Brick Road, and –

OZ'S VOICE   Quiet!

HICKORY   Ohhh!

Hickory runs back to Dorothy, Zeke and Hunk as they all tremble.

HICKORY   Ohhh.

Hunk almost faints with fear as Oz speaks. Hunk wobbles forward, salaams in front of the throne.

OZ'S VOICE   And you, Scarecrow, have the affrontery to ask for a brain – you billowing bale of bovine fodder!

HUNK   Y-Yes – Yes, Your Honour – I mean, Your Excellency – I – I mean – Your Wizardry!

OZ'S VOICE   Enough!

Hunk rises and runs back to the group.

OZ'S VOICE   Uhhh – and you – Lion!

Zeke groans with fear as he comes slowly forward.

OZ'S VOICE   Well?

Zeke tries to speak but faints, falling back. Dorothy and the others run forward to help him.

DOROTHY   Oh – oh – oh! [*she reacts*] You ought to be ashamed of yourself – frightening him like that, when he came to you for help!

OZ'S VOICE   Silence . . .! [*Dorothy and Hunk sit down as Oz continues*] . . . Whippersnapper! The beneficient Oz has every intention of granting your re- . . . [*Zeke revives and sits up. Dorothy starts to pull him up*] . . . quests!

ZEKE   What's that? What'd he say?

DOROTHY   Oh, come on.

ZEKE   Huh? What'd he say –

Dorothy helps Zeke to his feet and then the four of them listen as Oz speaks.

OZ'S VOICE   But first, you must prove yourselves worthy by performing a very small task. Bring me the broomstick of the Witch of the West.

HICKORY   B-B-B-B-But if we do that, we'll have to kill her to get it!

OZ'S VOICE   Bring me her broomstick and I'll grant your requests . . . [*Hunk, Zeke, Dorothy and Hickory tremble with fear*] . . . Now, go!

ZEKE   But – but what if she kills us first?

OZ'S VOICE   I said – Go!

Zeke jumps with fright, turns, and runs out of the throne room and into the corridor.

ZEKE   Ohhhh!

He runs forward and dives through the window to exit.

THE
HAUNTED
FOREST

The scene changes to the Haunted Forest. Weird trees surround the group and a signpost is seen:

Dorothy, Hunk, Hickory and Zeke walk forward through the forest and come upon the sign. Zeke reads it aloud then turns to go.

ZEKE [*reading aloud*] I'd turn back if I were you.

Two owls can be seen on the limb of a tree – Zeke turns to run but Hunk and Hickory run after him, bringing him back.

ZEKE [*crying for help*] Ohhhh, nooo, ohhhh-no!

Two crows on the limb of a tree blink their eyes.

HUNK   I believe there're spooks around here.

HICKORY   That's ridiculous! Spooks! That's silly.

ZEKE   But don't you believe in spooks?

> *Suddenly Hickory is lifted up out of the scene.*

HICKORY   No. Why only – oh!

DOROTHY   Oh! Oh, Tin Man!

> *Hickory falls back into the scene. Dorothy and Hunk rush forward.*

DOROTHY   Oh – oh –

HUNK   Oh – are you – are you all right?

> *Zeke trembles with fear, his eyes closed tight.*

ZEKE   I do believe in spooks. I do believe in spooks. I do – I do – I do – I do – I . . . [*Miss Gulch, Nikko and Winged Monkeys stand about in the Tower Room of her Castle. Miss Gulch paces around her throne, then instructs her Winged Monkeys, who fly out through the air. She stands at the window and bids them on.*] . . . I do believe in spooks. I do believe in spooks! I do – I do – I do – I do!

MISS GULCH [*laughing*] You'll believe in more than that before I'm finished with you. Take your army to the Haunted Forest, and bring me that girl and her dog. Do as you like with the others, but I want her alive and unharmed! They'll give you no trouble. I promise you that. I've sent a little insect on ahead to take the fight out of them. Take special care of those ruby slippers. I want those most of all. Now, fly! fly! fly! Bring me that girl and her slippers! Fly! Fly! Fly.

An army of Winged Monkeys fly over the Haunted Forest. Dorothy and the group see the monkeys approaching. They land and chase Dorothy, Hickory, Zeke and Hunk as they try to run away. Hickory swings his axe as the Monkeys try to capture him.

HICKORY   Go 'way now!

Winged Monkeys tromp on Hunk.

HUNK   Help! Help!

The Winged Monkeys grab Dorothy and fly off with her.

DOROTHY   Oh – oh – Oh!

Toto runs forward, looks up and barks. Another Winged Monkey picks him up, and the army of Winged Monkeys fly over the Haunted Forest and return to the castle.

Hunk is lying on the ground, yelling for help, and Zeke and Hickory start to put him together again.

HUNK   Help! Help! Help! Help!

HICKORY   Oh, well, what happened to you?

HUNK   They tore my legs off, and they threw them over there! Then they took my chest out and they threw it over there!

HICKORY   Well, that's you all over!

ZEKE   They sure knocked the stuffings out of you, didn't they?

HUNK   Don't stand there talking! Put me together! We've got to find Dorothy!

HICKORY   Now, let's see.

The scene is the Witch's Castle, perched high atop a mountainous rock. Inside Toto sits in Miss Gulch's lap. Dorothy is crying.

MISS GULCH   What a nice little dog. And you, my dear. What an unexpected pleasure. It's so kind of you to visit me in my loneliness.

DOROTHY   What are you going to do with my dog! Give him back to me!

Miss Gulch puts Toto in the basket and Nikko carries it away.

MISS GULCH   All in good time, my little pretty – all in good time.

DOROTHY   Oh, please give me back my dog!

MISS GULCH   Certainly – certainly – when you give me those slippers.

DOROTHY   But the Good Witch of the North told me not to.

MISS GULCH   Very well. Throw that basket in the river and drown him.

DOROTHY   No! No – No! Here, you can have your old slippers – but give me back Toto!

MISS GULCH   That's the good little girl. I knew you'd see reason!

Miss Gulch reaches down to touch the slippers but flames spark from the toe of one and her hands are quickly withdrawn.

MISS GULCH   [*screaming*] Ohhhh! Ohhh!

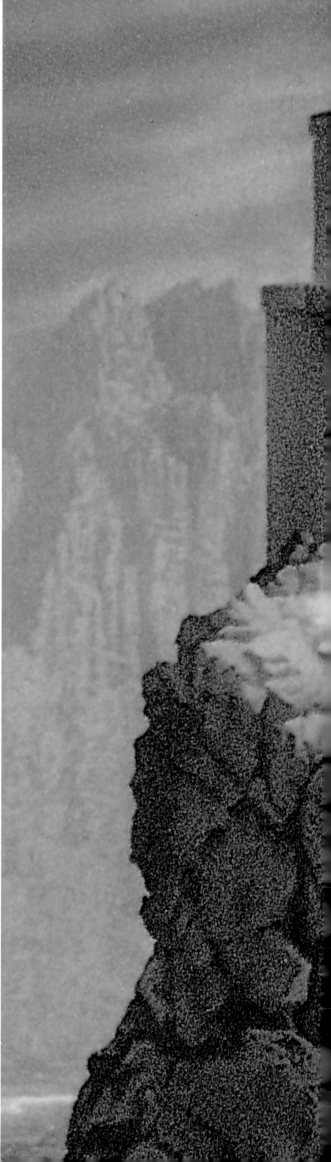

DOROTHY   I'm sorry, I didn't do it. Can I still have my dog?

MISS GULCH   No! Fool that I am. I should have remembered – those slippers will never come off, as long as you're alive. But's that's not what's worrying me. It's how to do it. These things must be done delicately . . . [*Toto sticks his head out of the basket*] . . . or you hurt the spell!

Toto jumps out of the basket and runs out of the door. Miss Gulch yells at Nikko to follow the dog.

DOROTHY   Run, Toto – run!

MISS GULCH   Catch him, you fool!

Toto runs down the hallway steps, with Nikko right behind him. He runs out to cross the moat as the drawbridge slowly goes up. Toto runs forward to the very tip of the bridge and looks over. Winkie guards run out of the castle, carrying spears. Toto jumps from the bridge, landing among the rocks.

DOROTHY   Run, Toto, run!

The Winkie guards throw their spears down at Toto from the drawbridge, but Toto escapes across the rocks with spears falling around him.

DOROTHY   Run, Toto, run! He got away! He got away!

Back in the Tower Room, Miss Gulch moves towards the hourglass.

MISS GULCH   Ohhhh! Which is more than you will! Drat you and your dog! You've been more trouble to me than you're worth, one way and another – but it'll soon be over now!

She picks up the hourglass and turns it upside down.

MISS GULCH   Do you see that? That's how much longer you've got to be
      alive! And it isn't long, my pretty – it isn't long! . . . [*She starts
      towards the door*] . . . I can't wait for ever to get those shoes!
      *Dorothy cries as the door closes and locks. She moves over to the
      throne and sits down by the crystal ball. Crying, she rests her head
      against the throne. Auntie Em's image appears in the crystal and
      she calls for Dorothy. Dorothy looks into the crystal.*

DOROTHY   I'm frightened, I'm frightened, Auntie Em – I'm frightened!
AUNTIE EM   Dorothy – Dorothy – where are you? It's me – it's Auntie Em.
      We're trying to find you! Where are you?
DOROTHY   I – I'm here in Oz, Auntie Em! I'm locked in the Witch's castle
      . . . and I'm trying to get home to you, Auntie Em! Oh, Auntie Em,
      don't go away! I'm frightened! Come back! Come back!
      Auntie Em fades out and the Witch fades into the crystal.
MISS GULCH   Auntie Em – Auntie Em – come back! I'll give you Auntie
      Em, my pretty [*laughing*].
      Sand runs rapidly into the lower half of the hourglass.

HUNK, ZEKE AND HICKORY TO THE RESCUE

*Outside the castle, among the rocks, Toto makes his way down to
the bottom of the mountain. He barks as he runs through the forest
to Hunk, Zeke and Hickory, who are working on putting Hunk
back together. Hickory hears Toto barking.*

HICKORY   Look! There's Toto! Where'd he come from?

Toto barks at the three.

HUNK   Why, don't you see? He's come to take us to Dorothy.

HICKORY   Oh –

HUNK   Come on, fellows!

*Hickory, Hunk and Zeke make their way over the rocky hillside
behind Toto, who barks as he waits for them. They struggle up the
rocks. Hickory slips off the ledge, hanging on to Zeke's tail to keep
from falling. Hunk tries to help.*

ZEKE   Oh, I – I – I hope my strength holds out.

HICKORY   I hope your tail holds out.

They approach the Witch's Castle.

ZEKE   What's that! What's that?

HUNK   That's the castle of the Wicked Witch!

*Hickory, Hunt, and Zeke peer over the rocks. Hickory starts to
cry.*

HUNK   Dorothy's in that awful place!

HICKORY   Oh, I hate to think of her in there. We've got to get her out!

HUNK   Don't cry now. We haven't got the oil can with us and you've been
        squeaking enough as it is.

ZEKE   Who's them? Who's them?

*The Witch's Winkies march about the castle courtyard as they
prepare to change guard. They chant.*

WINKIES   Yooo-hoo-hoo! Yo-ho!
          Yooo-hoo-hoo! Yo-ho!
          Yooo-hoo-hoo! Yo-ho!

*Outside the castle walls, Hickory, eke and Hunk peer over the
rocks.*

HUNK   I've got a plan how to get in there.

ZEKE   Fine. He's got a plan.

HUNK   And you're going to lead us.

ZEKE   Yeah. Me?

HUNK   Yes, you.

ZEKE   I – I – I – I – gotta get her out'a there?

HUNK   That's right.

ZEKE   All right, I'll go in there for Dorothy – Wicked Witch or no Wicked Witch – guards or no guards – I'll tear 'em apart. Ohhh! I may not come out alive but I'm going in there. There's only one thing I want you fellows to do.

HICKORY AND HUNK   What's that?

ZEKE   Talk me out of it.

HICKORY   No, you don't.

HUNK   Oh, no!

ZEKE   No? Now, wait a minute.

HICKORY   You don't neither –

HUNK   Up!

ZEKE   Now?

Sand trickles through to the lower part of the hourglass. Hunk, Zeke and Hickory, peering from behind the rocks, hear Toto barking and motion for him to be quiet. Three Winkie guards climb over the rocks towards them. The guards jump forward to seize the three. All disappear behind the rocks and as legs, arms and Zeke's tail fly about, they fight with the guards. Hickory, Hunk and Zeke then appear from behind the rocks in the Winkies' uniforms.

HUNK   Come on, I've got another idea.

ZEKE   Do – do you think it'll be polite – dropping in like this.

HICKORY   Come on – come on.

Hunk, Hickory and Zeke enter the castle courtyard as the Winkie guards march about. The three join the rear of the guards' line with Zeke trying to keep his tail under the uniform. Toto runs along behind as the line walks over the drawbridge and into the castle. The three duck behind a partition in the wall once the guards begin to exit right.

HICKORY   Where do we go now?

ZEKE   Yeah.

Toto barks on the steps of the castle tower and starts up the stairs.

HUNK   There!

Zeke, Hunk and Hickory follow Toto up the stairs in the Upper Hallway. Toto runs up to a door and starts to scratch at it.

HUNK   Wait! We'd better make sure. Dorothy, are you in there?

ZEKE   It's us!

DOROTHY   Yes, it's me! She's locked me in!

ZEKE   Listen, fellows. It's her. We gotta get her out! Open this door!

DOROTHY   Oh, hurry! Please hurry! . . . [*Sand continues to trickle into the lower half of the hourglass*] . . . The hourglass is almost empty!

HICKORY   Stand back.

With an axe they chop into the door. The upper section of the hourglass is almost empty. Dorothy runs free from the room. Hunk hands Toto to her.

DOROTHY   Oh – oh – oh, Toto! Toto!

ZEKE   Did they hurtcha?

DOROTHY   Lion – I knew you'd come!

HICKORY   Dorothy!

DOROTHY   I knew you would!

HUNK   Hurry, we've got no time to lose!

Dorothy, Hickory, Hunk and Zeke run down the stairs of the entrance hall. Huge doors swing shut in front of them but they cannot beat the doors. Miss Gulch laughs.

MISS GULCH   Going so soon? I wouldn't hear of it. Why, my little party's just beginning.

ZEKE   Trapped! Trapped like mice – er – rats?

Nikko and Miss Gulch hold up the hourglass and laugh. Toto, held in Dorothy's arms, barks as Winkie guards move forward slightly towards Hickory, Hunk, Dorothy and Zeke.

MISS GULCH   That's right. Don't hurt them right away. We'll let them think about it for a little first.

Hunk sees that a huge candelabra above Miss Gulch is secured by a rope running down the wall. He grabs Hickory's axe and cuts the rope to release the candelabra, which falls down upon the Winkies. Miss Gulch screams and throws the hourglass. It hits the floor and bursts into flames.

MISS GULCH   Seize them! Seize them! Seize them! There they go! Ah! Now we've got them! Half you go this way – half you go that way!

Hunk, Dorothy, Hickory and Zeke run to the top of the stairway.

MISS GULCH   Hurry! Hurry!

Dorothy, Hunk, Hickory and Zeke run downstairs from the tower and along the battlements. They stop and look around.

ZEKE   Where do we go now?

HUNK   This way – come on!

They run across the battlements to the right but stop at the stairs
leading to the tower as a group of Winkies chase down the steps,
yelling.

HUNK Back! Back!

The group run left along the battlements with Winkies following
them. Other Winkies enter from the left and surround them. They
are terrorised and rush forward to stand against the railings. Miss
Gulch enters, followed by Nikko.

MISS GULCH Well! Ring around the Rosey! A pocket full of spears!
Thought you'd be pretty foxy, didn't you? Well, the last to go will see
the first three go before her! And your mangy little dog, too!

Miss Gulch grins as she lifts her broom to a burning torch on the
wall. The broomstick catches fire.

MISS GULCH How about a little fire, Scarecrow? Huh?

The burning broomstick touches Hunk's arm. He jumps up and
down yelling. Dorothy puts Toto down and grabs a bucket of
water.

HUNK No! No! No! No! Help! I'm burning! I'm burning! I'm burning!

Dorothy screams and throws the water towards Hunk, but it
splashes over Miss Gulch instead. She screams because she begins
to melt away, leaving her cloak and hat in a heap on the floor with
smoke rising from it.

MISS GULCH Ohhh! You cursed brat! Look what you've done! I'm
melting! Melting! Oh, what a world! What a world! Who would have
thought a good little girl like you could destroy my beautiful wicked-
ness? Ohhh! Look out! Look out! I'm going. Ohhh – Ohhhhhhhhh!

Zeke, Hickory, Dorothy and Hunk look on in amazement as Miss Gulch's cloak and hat smoulder on the floor. Toto paws at the remains. Nikko looks down at it. The Leader of the Winkies steps forward.

LEADER OF WINKIES   She's – she's dead. You've killed her.

DOROTHY   I didn't mean to kill her – really I didn't. It's – it's just that he was on fire!

The Leader addresses the Winkies and they all go down on their knees to Dorothy.

LEADER   Hail to Dorothy! The Wicked Witch is dead!

WINKIES   Hail! Hail to Dorothy! The Wicked Witch is dead!

DOROTHY   The broom!

The Leader gives the broomstick to Dorothy.

DOROTHY   May we have it!

LEADER   Please. And take it with you.

DOROTHY   Oh, thank you so much! Now we can go back to the Wizard and tell him the Wicked Witch is dead!

WINKIES   The Wicked Witch is dead!

THE WIZARD KEEPS HIS PROMISES

The scene now returns to the interior Throne Room in the Palace of the Wizard. The image of Oz is seen above the throne and Dorothy, Hunk, Zeke and Hickory stand before it.

OZ'S VOICE   Can I believe my eyes? Why have you come back?
Dorothy steps forward and puts the broomstick on the floor.

DOROTHY   Please, sir. We've done what you told us. We've brought you the broomstick of the Wicked Witch of the West. We melted her.

OZ'S VOICE   Oh – you liquidated her, eh? Very resourceful!

DOROTHY   Yes, sir. So we'd like you to keep your promise to us – if you please, sir.

OZ'S VOICE   Not so fast! Not so fast! I'll have to give the matter a little thought! Go away, and come back tomorrow!

DOROTHY   Tomorrow! Oh, but I want to go home now!

HICKORY   You've had plenty of time already!

ZEKE   Yeah!
Flames and smoke flare from the Throne of Oz.

OZ'S VOICE   Do not arouse the wrath of the . . . [*Toto runs to a curtain hanging around the side of the throne*] . . . Great and Powerful Oz! I said come back tomorrow!

DOROTHY   If you were really great and powerful, you'd keep your promises!

OZ'S VOICE   Do you presume to criticise the Great . . .
Toto pulls the curtain aside to show the Professor working the controls, and speaking into a microphone.

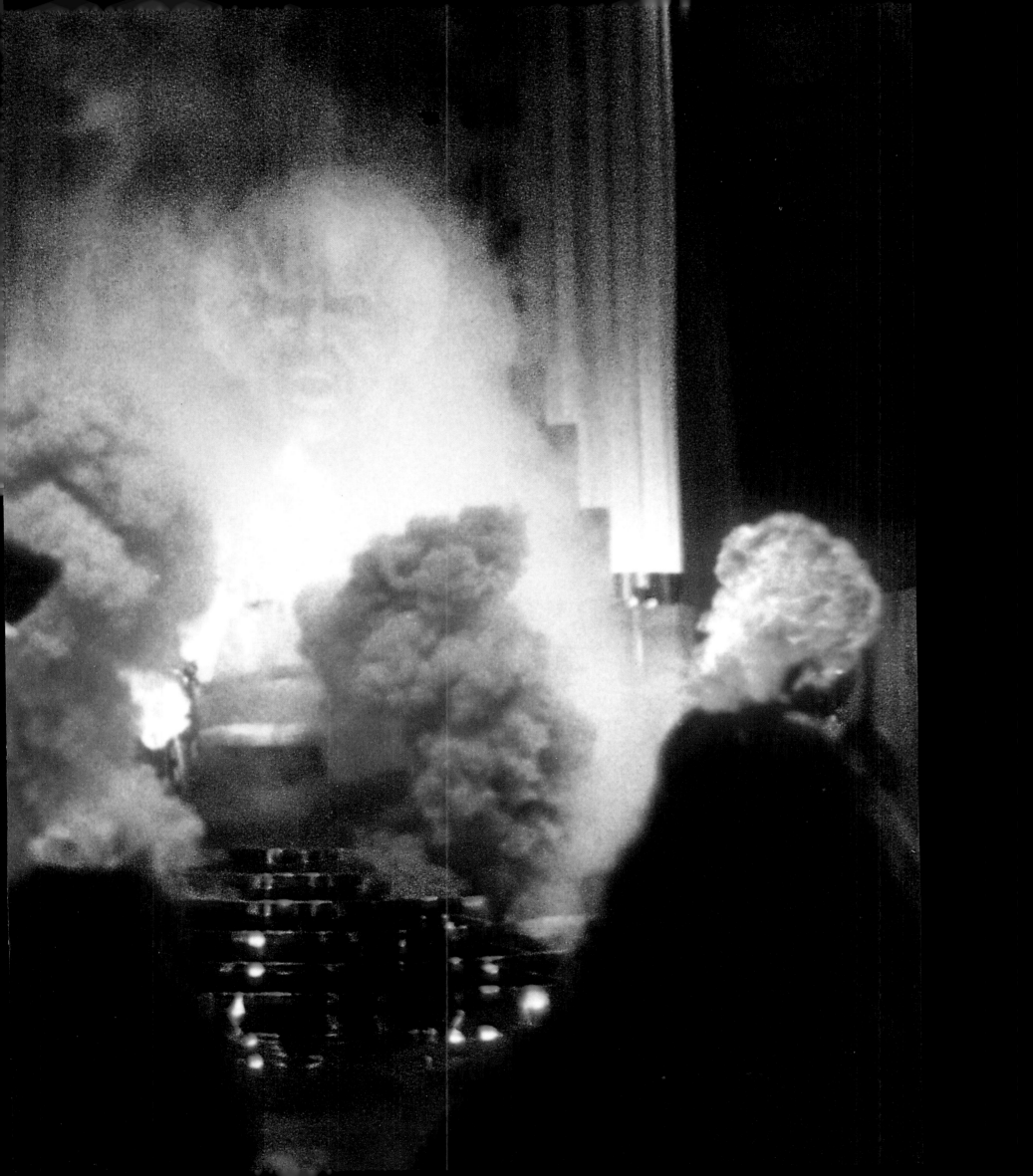

OZ'S VOICE (PROFESSOR) . . . Oz? You ungrateful creatures! Think yourselves lucky that I'm giving you an audience tomorrow, instead of . . . [*Dorothy and the group have been watching the Professor working the controls on the throne. Professor turns to speak into the microphone and realises he can be seen. He pulls the curtain back into place hurriedly*] . . . twenty years from now! Oh! The Great Oz has spoken! Oh! Pay no attention to that man behind the curtain. The Great . . . [*Dorothy pulls the curtain aside again, revealing the Professor*] . . . Powerful – has spoken –

DOROTHY Who are you?

PROFESSOR Well, I – I – I am the Great and Powerful – Wizard of Oz.

DOROTHY You are?

PROFESSOR Uh –

DOROTHY I don't believe you!

PROFESSOR No, I'm afraid it's true. There's no other Wizard except me.

HUNK You humbug!

ZEKE Yeah!

PROFESSOR Yes – that's exactly so – I'm a humbug.

DOROTHY Oh – you're a very bad man!

PROFESSOR Oh, no, my dear. I – I'm a very good man. I'm just a very bad Wizard.

HUNK What about the heart that you promised the Tin Man?

PROFESSOR Well, I –

HUNK And the courage you promised Cowardly Lion?

PROFESSOR Well, I –

HICKORY AND ZEKE And Scarecrow's brain?

PROFESSOR Why, anybody can have a brain. That's a very mediocre commodity. Every pusillanimous creature that crawls on the earth, or slinks through slimy seas has a brain! Back where I come from we have universities – seats of great learning – where men go to become great thinkers. And when they come out, they think deep thoughts, and with no more brains than you have. But – they have one thing you haven't got – a diploma!

Professor picks up several diplomas, selects one and presents it to Hunk.

PROFESSOR Therefore, by virtue of the authority vested in me by the Universita Committeeatum a pluribus unum, I hereby confer upon you the honorary degree of Th.D.

HUNK Th.D.?

PROFESSOR Yeah – that – that's Dr. of Thinkology.

Hunk puts his hand to his head.

HUNK The sum of the square roots of any two sides of an isosceles triangle is equal to the square root of the remaining side. Oh, joy! Rapture! I've got a brain! How can I ever thank you enough?

Professor steps over to Zeke and opens his black bag, taking out a medal.

PROFESSOR   Well, you can't. As for you, my fine friend, you are a victim of disorganised thinking. You are under the unfortunate delusion that simply because you run away from danger you have no courage!·You are confusing courage with wisdom. Back where I come from we have men who are called heroes. Once a year they take their fortitude out of mothballs and parade it down the main street of the city. And they have no more courage than you have. But – they have one thing that you haven't got! A medal! Therefore, for meritorious . . . [*Professor pins the medal on Zeke.*] . . . conduct, extraordinary valor, conspicuous bravery against wicked witches, I award you the Triple Cross. You are now a member of the Legion of Courage!

Professor kisses Zeke on one cheek, and then the other.

ZEKE   Oh – oh, shucks, folks – I'm speechless!

PROFESSOR   As for you, my galvanized friend – you want a heart! You don't know how lucky you are not to have one. Hearts will never be practical until they can be made unbreakable.

HICKORY   But I – I still want one.

PROFESSOR   Back where I come from there are men who do nothing all day but good deeds. They are called phil . . . er . . phil . . . er . . er . . . good-deed-doers and their hearts are no bigger than yours, but they have one thing you haven't got! A testimonial!

Professor takes a heart-shaped watch from his black bag and presents it to Hickory.

PROFESSOR   Therefore, in consideration of your kindness, I take pleasure at this time in presenting you with a small token of our esteem and affection. And remember, my sentimental friend, that a heart is not judged by how much you love, but by how much you are loved by others.

Hickory listens to his watch and holds it to Dorothy's ear.

HICKORY   Oh. Oh, it ticks! Listen! Look, it ticks!

ZEKE   Read – read what my medal says. Courage! Ain't it the truth!

DOROTHY   Oh – oh, they're all wonderful.

HUNK   Hey, what about Dorothy?

HICKORY   Yes, how about Dorothy?

ZEKE   Yeah.

PROFESSOR   A –

ZEKE   Dorothy next!

PROFESSOR   Yes, Dorothy. A –

DOROTHY   Oh, I don't think there's anything in that black bag for me.

PROFESSOR   Well – you force me into a cataclysmic decision. The only way to get Dorothy back to Kansas is for me to take her there myself!

DOROTHY   Oh! Oh, will you? Could you? Oh! Oh, but are you a clever enough wizard to manage it?

PROFESSOR   Child, you cut me to the quick! I'm an old Kansas man myself, born and bred – in the heart of the western wilderness, premier balloonist *par excellence*. I was engaged by the Miracle Wonderland Carnival Company, only one day, while performing spectacular feats of stratospheric skill never before attempted by civilised man, an unfortunate phenomena occurred – the balloon failed to return to the fair.

ZEKE   It did!

DOROTHY   Weren't you frightened?

PROFESSOR   Frightened? You are talking to a man who has laughed in the face of death, sneered at doom, chuckled at castastrophe! I was petrified. Then suddenly the wind changed and the balloon floated down into the heart of this noble city where I was instantaneously acclaimed Oz, the first Wizard deluxe.

DOROTHY   Ahhh!

PROFESSOR   Times being what they were, I accepted the job, retaining my balloon against the advent of a quick get-away. Aha! And in that balloon, my dear Dorothy, you and I will return to the Land of A Pluribus Unum!

Dorothy shows her delight.

FAREWELL TO OZ

The scene moves to the Street of Oz where the Balloon is in place ready for departure. The people of Oz are gathered around the platform and throughout the street. There is great cheering and celebration.

PROFESSOR   This is positively the finest exhibition ever to be shown . . . well, be that as it may. I, your Wizard, par adua outer, am about to embark on a hazardous and technically unexplainable journey into the outer stratosphere.

The crowd surround the balloon, cheering.

PROFESSOR   To confer, converse and otherwise hob-nob with my brother wizards. And I hereby decree that until what time, if any, that I return, the Scarecrow by virtue of his highly superior brains, shall rule in my stead, assisted by the Tin Man, by virtue of his magnificent heart, and the Lion by virtue of his courage! Obey them as you would me.

Toto, in Dorothy's arms, barks at something out of sight.

. . . Thank You.

An Oz woman stands holding a cat in her arms. The cat howls and Toto jumps down, disappearing after the cat. Dorothy starts to climb out of the basket as Toto barks in pursuit of the cat.

DOROTHY   Oh, Toto – come back! Toto! Toto! [*Dorothy climbs out of the basket and runs past Hunk and Zeke down the steps*] . . . Oh, don't go without me! I'll be right back! Toto!
Hunk and Zeke hold the ropes of the balloon, but are distracted and exit right after Dorothy.

HICKORY   Stop that dog!

PROFESSOR   This is a highly irregular procedure! This is absolutely unprecedented!

HICKORY   Help! Help! The balloon's going up!!

PROFESSOR   Ruined . . . [*The balloon starts to rise with the Professor in the basket. Hickory tries to hold it down. Dorothy and Zeke run back up onto the platform. The Professor waves to the people below and they wave back*] . . . my exit!

DOROTHY   Oh! Come back! Come back! Don't go without me! Please come back!

PROFESSOR: I can't come back! I don't know how it works! Goodbye, folks!

PEOPLE   Goodbye! Goodbye! Goodbye! Goodbye!
Dorothy, holding Toto, is comforted.

DOROTHY   Oh, now I'll never get home!

ZEKE   Stay with us, then, Dorothy. We all love you. We don't want you to go.

DOROTHY   Oh, that's very kind of you, but this could never be like Kansas. Auntie Em must have stopped wondering what happened to me by now. Oh, Scarecrow, what am I going to do?

HUNK   Look! Here's someone who can help you.

A giant bubble appears and floats towards the platform. A group of Oz men bow and exit right and left as the bubble floats down. Glinda appears from it. She waves her wand. Dorothy, holding Toto, curtsies.

DOROTHY   Oh – will you help me? Can you help me?

GLINDA   You don't need to be helped any longer. You've always had the power to go back to Kansas.

DOROTHY   I have?

HUNK   Then why didn't you tell her before?

GLINDA   Because she wouldn't have believed me. She had to learn it for herself.

HICKORY   What have you learned, Dorothy?

DOROTHY   Well, I – I think that it – that it wasn't enough just to want to see Uncle Henry and Auntie Em. And it's that – if I ever go looking for my heart's desire again, I won't look any further than my own backyard, because if it isn't there, I never really lost it to begin with. Is that right?

GLINDA   That's all it is!

HUNK   But that's so easy! I should have thought of it for you.

HICKORY   I should have felt it in my heart.

GLINDA   No. She had to find it out for herself. Now those magic slippers will take you home in two seconds!

DOROTHY   Oh!

Dorothy goes to Hickory, wipes his tears from his eyes and hands him his oil can, kissing him on the cheek. She kisses Zeke and

embraces Hunk and kisses him. She crosses to Glinda, then turns
to the left and waves Toto's paw.

DOROTHY Toto, too?

GLINDA Toto, too.

DOROTHY Oh, now?

GLINDA Whenever you wish.

DOROTHY Oh, dear, that's too wonderful to be true! Oh, it's – it's going to
be so hard to say goodbye. I love you all, too. Goodbye Tin Man. Oh,
don't cry. You rust so dreadfully. Here, here's your oil can. Goodbye.

HICKORY Now I know I've got a heart, 'cause it's breaking.

DOROTHY Oh. Goodbye, Lion. You know, I know it isn't right, but I'm
gonna miss the way you used to holler for help before you found your
courage.

ZEKE Well, I would never've found it if it hadn't been for you.

DOROTHY I think I'll miss you most of all.

GLINDA Are you ready now?

DOROTHY Yes. Say goodbye, Toto. Yes, I'm ready now.

GLINDA Then close your eyes and tap your heels together three times.
Glinda waves her wand and Dorothy clicks her shoes together
three times. She closes her eyes and we see a spiral effect.

GLINDA And think to yourself. 'There's no place like home. There's no
place like home'.

DOROTHY AND GLINDA There's no place like home. There's no place like
home.

DOROTHY There's no place like home. There's no place like home.
There's no place like home.

THERE'S NO PLACE LIKE HOME

The house appears and falls downward through space, landing with a crash. Inside the farmhouse, Dorothy is resting on a pillow, mumbling to herself with her eyes closed. Auntie Em places a cloth on Dorothy's forehead.

DOROTHY There's no place like home. There's no place like home. There's no place . . . .

Dorothy opens her eyes. Auntie Em is sitting on the bed beside her and Uncle Henry is standing at the right. Auntie Em removes the cloth from Dorothy's head.

AUNTIE EM Wake up, honey.

DOROTHY There's no place like home. There's no place like home. No place . . . .

AUNTIE EM Dorothy. Dorothy, dear, It's Aunt Em, darling.

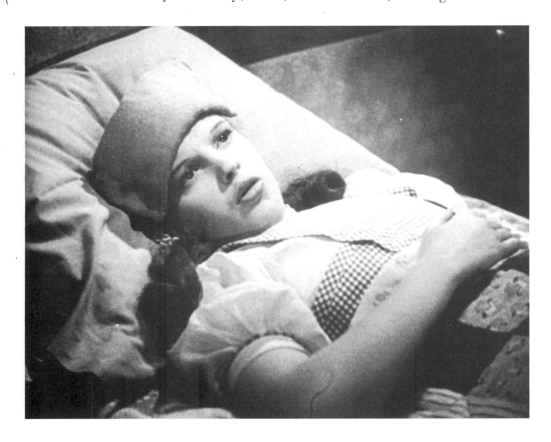

DOROTHY   Oh, Auntie Em, it's you!

AUNTIE EM   Yes, darling.

Professor pops his head in at the window.

PROFESSOR   Hello, there! Anybody home? I – just dropped by because I heard the little girl got caught in the big – Well – she seems all right now.

UNCLE HENRY   Yes. She got quite a bump on the head. We kind of thought there for a minute she was gonna leave us.

PROFESSOR   Oh.

DOROTHY   But I did leave you, Uncle Henry. That's just the trouble. And I tried to get back for days and days.

AUNTIE EM   There, there, lie quiet now. You just had a bad dream.

DOROTHY   No.

Hunk, Hickory and Zeke enter the room to see Dorothy.

HUNK   Sure. Remember me, you old pal, Hunk?

DOROTHY   Oh.

HICKORY   And me, Hickory?

ZEKE   You couldn't forget my face, could you?

DOROTHY   No. But it wasn't a dream. It was a place. And you – and you and you – and you were there.

PROFESSOR   Oh!

DOROTHY   But you couldn't have been, could you?

AUNTIE EM   Oh, we dream lots of silly things when we –

DOROTHY   No, Aunt Em, this was a real, truly live place. And I remember that some of it wasn't very nice – but most of it was beautiful. But just the same, all I kept saying to everybody was, 'I want to go home!' And they sent me home.

Dorothy sits in the bed with Auntie Em near her. The Professor looks in at the window. Uncle Henry, Hunk, Zeke and Hickory are gathered around. Toto jumps upon to the bed and Dorothy hugs him.

DOROTHY   Doesn't anybody believe me?

UNCLE HENRY   Of course we believe you, Dorothy.

DOROTHY   Oh, but anyway, Toto, we're home! Home! And this is my room – and you're all here! And I'm not going to leave here ever, ever again, because I love you all! And – Oh, Auntie Em, there's no place like home!

End

C A S T

Dorothy..JUDY GARLAND

Professor Marvel.. FRANK MORGAN

"Hunk".. RAY BOLGER

"Zeke".. BERT LAHR

"Hickory"... JACK HALEY

Glinda.. BILLIE BURKE

Miss Gulch....................................MARGARET HAMILTON

Uncle Henry .... CHARLEY GRAPEWIN

Nikko.. PAT WALSHE

Auntie Em .... CLARA BLANDICK

Toto.. TOTO

The Singer Midgets as The Munchkins

Screen Play by
NOEL LANGLEY, FLORENCE RYERSON and EDGAR ALLAN WOOLF

Adaptation by Noel Langley

From the book by L. Frank Baum

MUSICAL PROGRAMME

Adaptation by
HERBERT STOTHART

Lyrics by   Music by

E. Y. HARBURG   HAROLD ARLEN

Associate Conductor	George Stoll
Orchestral and Vocal Arrangements.........	George Bassman
	Murray Cutter
	Paul Marquardt
	Ken Darby

Musical Numbers staged by Bobby Connolly

Photographed in Technicolor by	Harold Rosson, A.S.C.
Associate..	Allen Davey, A.S.C.
Technicolor Colour Director	Natalie Kalmus
Associate..	Henri Jaffa
Recording Director	Douglas Shearer
Art Director......................................	Cedric Gibbons
Associate.......................................	William A. Horning
Set Decorations..............................	Edwin B. Willis
Special Effects	Arnold Gillespie
Costumes by......................................	Adrian
Character Make-Ups created by.............	Jack Dawn
Film Editor.......................................	Blanche Sewell

WESTERN ELECTRIC SOUND SYSTEM (Trade Mark)

M.F.P.D.A. Seal   I.A.T.S.E.
Certificate No. 5464   Insignia